Coaching The Unemployable
Don't Resign Just Re-sign

Michael Gatewood

Luke 10:7 "...and in the same house remain, eating and drinking such things as they give: for the laborer is worthy of his hire. Go not from house to house..."

For more information or to order additional books please email or call:

WOODGATE
SYSTEMATIC LEADERSHIP IDEALS
~Developing Champion Solutions that work ~

954-358-9425

mgpublication@gmail.com
www.michaelgatewoodslifeline.blogspot.com

DEDICATION

I give this book to all the employers who gave me a chance ,and to the employees who met the challenge of working with me. Thank you for teaching me, now I will share our moments together with the world! "…Silver and gold I have not; but what I have, this give I to thee: In the name of Jesus Christ the Nazaraean rise up and walk". Acts 3:6

Personal Disclaimer:

If in your journey you find the ideas, suggestions, and information in this book are not proving to be effective, then you may need to evaluate your technique because the bible texts and the biblical principles presented here are flawless. The information in this book is to be considered advice based on entrepreneurs and employee experiences. This is not legal or medical advice if this is what you are in need of. Please get help from a licensed professional. If you have any issues with the book please return to distributer for a refund. God don't want your money, just your heart.

CONTENTS

Acknowledgments   i

1   A WORD FROM MIKE G   1

2   15 WEEKS TO RECOVERY   3

3   EMPLOYMENT MATTERS   62

4   CAREER JUICE   69

5   MASTER PLAN   79

6   THE INTERVIEW   93

7   JOBS IN THE BIBLE   101

8   AGGREMENTS & EVALUATIONS   110

9   THE MAN, MINISTRY, & LEGACY   125

10   SPECIAL OFFER   130

ACKNOWLEDGMENTS

Thank you God for all the wisdom you have imparted to me. Thank you www.butlerworks.com for the jokes added to the book. Thank you Cassandra A. Gibson for pushing me in to my new career. Thank you Sheila C. Fagan for being my friend and taking care of my kids when I could not. Thank you Jim R. Brown for teaching me about people. Thank you Chester C. Price for teaching me about loyalty. Thank you Eddie Valentine for teaching me how to hustle. Thank you Patricia K. Miller for teaching me that it's O.K. to be tough and shed a tear every now and then. Thank you Robert Allen for teaching me it's not what you say; it's what I do that's important. Thank you Ben Cotheren for teaching me about accountability. Thank you Chris (Black) Cheshire for believing in me. Thank you Julie Gomez for treating me like a son. Thank you Judy Krouse for giving me a second chance. Thank you James Jefferson for teaching me integrity and being my best man. Thank you Dale Green for helping me at the Workforce center and last but not least, I am very proud of the leaders I have trained: Renee, Jennifer, Ronnie, and Lorena (because even though it was rough, you hung in until the end).

CHAPTER ONE A WORD FROM MIKE G

The reason I wrote this book is to give people who are un-employable a chance to change the world. In January 2008, the Bureau of Labor Statistics stated that the unemployment rate was 5.9%, and not just in different parts of the world, but in Florida where I live. So I embarked on a task of writing a book that tells you how to keep your job or pursue a better one. There are so many books that tell you how to get a job. I figured since unemployment is on an incline, I needed to get involved! So I decided to write a book that will expose you to the grace within your current job and propel you to your new career. This book will not make you rich, but it will enrich your life. I'm 36 years old, and I've worked for U-Save, Burger King (7x), Mc Donald's (4x), Eckerd's, Arby's, Ponderosa, Pizza Hut, Kentucky Fried Chicken (4x), Kenny Rodger's Roasters, Hardee's, Humana Hospital, City of Tampa, Signature Group, Wal* Mart, Churches, Walgreen's (2x), Waffle House (3x), Taco Bell, Wendy's (5x), Circle K, Department of Insurance, and the Seven Eleven. With all the jobs I have kept and pursued, I would like to believe I am an expert. The truth is that none of us are because the work force is constantly changing. Now, if you pay attention your job history will not be as long as mine. Going from job to job is not only hard on you but it affects your family and the employer. The secret to seeking a career is this: the things you Value are the Vehicles that will keep you at work! Know what you value, because "where your heart is there your treasure will be also." I decided at my last job that I needed to do what I love, so I became self-employed and started writing. This country has so many resources, but you have to do your research. Just like school isn't for everybody, some jobs aren't either. Remember: what doesn't enhance you could indelibly entrap you! Experience the workforce as we co-labor together.

. Moving forward let's talk about the book!

In Coaching The Un Employ able: Don't Resign; Just Re-sign, Michael Gatewood explains how to get through job disparities, by using compelling examples from others' and his own life experiences. This book is designed to help you consider a career for your life. Michael Gatewood outlines a simple but powerful strategy to help you identify work ethics and live them to the fullest. This strategy is composed of two intricate parts:

Fifteen Weeks of Devotion: A composition of Parables, Quotes and Queries, and Psalms for the work place - this section is designed to lead you to the top at work.
Employment Matters: This section of the book walks you through the job search and talks you through the interview to eventually becoming the supervisor. You learn just how much legwork and handy work are involved. "If you get involved you will evolve."

If you are constantly devoting your passions to the challenges in your life, you will never truly realize the purpose that changes your life. It is my desire that you will be confident as you strive to make a difference in your chosen career and that you will execute these steps faithfully with all your heart
I pray that when you finish this volume of Coaching the Un Employ able, you will have a profound respect for what you do and continue with unwavering dedication and boundless energy to deal with seemingly endless problems and crises. Although your job may be difficult, it is not impossible if you believe. I pray this blueprint for success will make your workplace a worship place, provided you Don't Resign Just Re – sign.

You can do this!, if you can't do it for yourself neither will anyone else! Don't just read this book (Buy It) .Invest in yourself. Don't just invest get involved. "It's okay if you won't invest you just not interested in much success.

CHAPTER TWO 15 WEEKS TO RECOVERY

WEEK ONE: DON'T START WHAT YOU CAN'T FINISH

This day is for people who are ready. The first week we call you in. No complaints. We ask you to do extra work, much more than your share. No Complaints. You come to work early. No Complaints. Your uniform is so crisp, it'll stand up without you. The first week is over. But guess what? All that stuff you did in the beginning is still expected of you. The question is: will hold up or fold up? There are several lessons to be learned from this. Number one: *"First impressions can be your last expression."* Only God looks at the heart; man looks at the outward appearance. When you can do great things, greatness is expected of you.

Revelation 22:12   and, behold, I come quickly; and my reward [is] with me, to give every man according as his work shall be.

Isaiah 3:10 Say ye to the righteous, that [it shall be] well [with him]: for they shall eat the fruit of their doings.

It's better to be a superstar at home because work appreciation depreciates with time. That's why I've learned to *"Do what's required, not what's inspired."* So many of us go above and beyond the call of duty when it comes to work, when all they really want is for us to follow instructions. But we want to be the first to be recognized, so we do more than our share. The book of life says, "the first shall be last and the last shall be first." Maybe it's not your turn to be noticed. Get in the habit of following your job assignment. If you don't have one, make one and be sure you cross off what's completed. If a task is not completed, put a reason why. Then, no one can say it wasn't done. It also shows that you were productive if you have more than three things listed. Remember: when making your list, there should be something to do every hour that you work. This gives you discipline and shows productivity

ACTIVITY:

"IF YOU NEVER HAVE BAD DAYS, YOU'LL NEVER KNOW WHEN THE GOOD DAYS COME."

1. How does this apply in your life?

2. Who can you share this with that needs it?

3. What is your idea of the worst day?

4. Now what can you do to make the best of #3?

5. Now vow to find a compliment within every complaint

Focus Thought:

"And Nehemiah, which [is] the Tirshatha, and Ezra the priest the scribe, and the Levites that taught the people, said unto all the people, This day [is] holy unto the LORD your God; mourn not, nor weep. For all the people wept, when they heard the words of the law"

*"Then he said unto them, Go your way, eat the fat, and drink the sweet, and send portions unto them for whom nothing is prepared: for [this] day [is] holy unto our Lord: neither be ye sorry; **for the joy of the LORD is your strength."***

Nehemiah 8:9-10

Coach's Corner

- When you're having a bad day, think about the alternative: you could be dead!

- The things we put off fall on other people

The average interview last 55minutes/management level 86 minutes – Robert Half Recruitment

Always be Cozy

Cozy :giving a feeling of comfort, warmth, and relaxation.

" Don't you get mad, make others mad about you"

Your environment may not be rosy, but you can still be cozy. For he who is temperate shall receive more grace than he who loses his temper and falls on his face.

Don't be impressed by the stress. Just do your very best. Be you no matter what there is to do. It's o.k. to say no; life is still a go!

It's o.k. to be hospitable, even when you're miserable. Nothing can ever frustrate you, as long as you appreciate what you do.

So keep a steady pace and put a smile upon your face. You don't have to fit in to get in. This will not help you to win. Why settle for less when you deserve the best? If it is really not you, nothing else will do until you see things through.

Your life is just a test of how much you will invest towards your own success.

Your environment may not be rosy, but you can still be cozy. For he who is temperate shall receive more grace than he who loses his temper and falls on his face.

WEEK TWO: IT AINT MY FAULT !

A lot of us are good-hearted; we open ourselves to the slaughter. We are so responsible that we start making decisions on the job. One day, your boss doesn't catch the vision, so he alters your blueprint for success. Watch out! I sense a great distress in the workforce. Why are you possessing another man's dream? When you work for people, stop putting in work orders, and just do the work.

Hebrews 13:17   Obey them that have the rule over you, and submit yourselves: for they watch for your souls, as they that must give account, that they may do it with joy, and not with grief: for that [is] unprofitable for you.

It's great you want to be responsible, but ultimately the responsibility falls on them. Relax. God is still on the throne. It's hard to let go when you care about what you do, but just remember in letting go, you let God take control. To do anything else would be disobedient to God's Word, and in the work force, it's almost like wrestling with yourself. Who wants to get hit in the eye twice? Don't stop caring about what you do for others because what you do for others will identify who you are. A "person who doesn't care is a careless person." (author unknown) The greatest servant in life is not one who works in the fire, but the one who works while under fire.

Luke 8:22-25
Now it came to pass on a certain day, that he went into a ship with his disciples: and he said unto them, Let us go over unto the other side of the lake. And they launched forth.
But as they sailed he fell asleep: and there came down a storm of wind on the lake; and they were filled [with water], and were in jeopardy.
And they came to him, and awoke him, saying, Master, master, we perish. Then he arose, and rebuked the wind and the raging of the water: and they ceased, and there was a calm.
And he said unto them, Where is your faith? And they being afraid wondered, saying one to another, what manner of man is this! For he commandeth even the winds and water, and they obey him.

Don't worry be happy! You only have to be responsible for your actions, and the rest is up to those you work for. Rest easy. No matter what goes up or what comes down, sing it with me now - "It ain't my fault!" Now, you can only claim this phrase when you are submissive to authority. Otherwise, it is your fault. A lot of times we ask for God to be our intercessor, but we get in the way. Doubt can blind you to the truth, so keep the faith.

ACTIVITY:

"FIRST IMPRESSION, LAST EXPRESSION"

1. Can you recall a time when you gave the wrong impression?

2. The impression may be but a moment, but the expression lasts a lifetime.
   Explain these statements.

3. Are you doing your best to be the best?

4. Will you commit to positive impressions to prompt motivated expressions?

Focus Thought:

"While we look not at the things, which are seen, but at the things which are not seen: for the things, which are seen [are] temporal; but the things, which are not seen [are] eternal."

II Corinthians 4:18

Coach's Corner

- The best impression you can give is to be genuine
- Whatsoever things are pure, kind, and true..
- If you don't have the smarts, at least look the part

If you're shy or quiet , you're not alone introverts outnumber extroverts 50.8% to 49.3%. More men are introverts 54.1% than women 47.5% -Fortune Magazine

Always be Creative

Creative: relating to or involving the imagination or original ideas, especially in the production of an artistic work

Creativity is the key to escaping your own captivity. You must discover your needs, and if you have any seeds, then plant some, save some, and be careful of the weeds.

When times are cold, you still must be bold. When the action stops, you're still racing the clock. Now, the market is competitive in all that you do. But nothing can compare to the talent within you. Don't hide your talent when things unglue. After all, people are depending on you.

Creativity is the key to escaping your own captivity. You must discover your needs, and if you have any seeds, plant some, save some, and be careful of the weeds.

We can sell everyone else except ourselves. We don't believe we are worthy because our speech is not too wordy. If your talent is abused or often not used, one day you may lose, if you do not choose. You must rise through adversity through Life University. It's all about initiative and being creative.

Creativity is the key to escaping your own captivity. You must discover your needs, and if you have any seeds, plant some, save some, and be careful of the weeds.

II Corinthians 12:8-11
For to one is given by the Spirit the word of wisdom; to another the word of knowledge by the same Spirit;
To another faith by the same Spirit; to another the gifts of healing by the same Spirit;
To another the working of miracles; to another prophecy; to another discerning of spirits; to another [divers] kinds of tongues; to another the interpretation of tongues:
But all these worketh that one and the selfsame Spirit, dividing to every man severally as he will.

WEEK THREE SAY MY NAME,SAY MY NAME!

"A job identifies what you do; but a career defines who you are."

~ Michael Gatewood

Ecclesiastes 7:1 - a good name [is] better than precious ointment; and the day of death than the day of one's birth.

People love hearing their name or title. There is nothing wrong with that if you've earned it, but most of us want the glory, but have no guts. People are not called Pastor or Doctor because they like it. They had to work hard for their title, so why shouldn't you. People don't care about how long you've been in. The skill doesn't matter as much as the will. Personally, I want people to associate my name with my career and not the other way around. Just think back; for others, think way back when you were a kid. Did your mom or dad read the bible to you, lived it, and poured it in to you? When you die, what do you think your kids will remember about you: your status or salvation? It's good to be career minded; however, strength of character is everything and the courage to be faithful is almost extinct. Find out what your name means and try to live up to it. You can use the online etymology dictionary at www.etymologyonline.com

What does your name mean?

Now take a minute and make every letter in your name mean something.

Now, every day I want you to memorize this until you can recite it from memory, along with three scriptures. Why three? Two should coincide with your first and/or last name's meaning, and the third is your personal commitment to God and self.

ACTIVITY:

Why complain, you'll just think about the problem more"

1. What's your problem today?

2. Have you thought about the alternatives?

3. Do you like the problems you're having?

4. Have you thought about a solution?

5. What is the solution?

Focus Thought:

Philippians 4:11

"Not that I speak in respect of want: for I have learned, in whatsoever state I am, [therewith] to be content."

Coach's Corner

- Everybody has problems, but it doesn't mean
  You have to be a problem too.

- If you need someone to talk to, email me at:
  mgpublication@gmail.com (Coach, for subject)
- Confession is good for the soul, but bad for the career

55% of another person's perception of you is based on how you look –Image Dynamics

Always be Clement (tolerant)

Opposites attract, diversity is attacked, prejudice is back, and I thought it never left because I feel singled out and all by myself

They're not like me. How can this be? I can do a little of this and a lot of that. Why on earth can they stay on the track? The knowledge I receive is all that I believed. They have more college than me. They play on words in efforts to deceive. Have mercy on me. What a great controversy. All I see is adversity. They say it's a matter of diversity.

Opposites attract, diversity is attacked, prejudice is back, and I thought it never left because I feel singled out and all by myself

We all have different talents, weaknesses and gifts. It's not just a myth. We need to serve one another and not hate each other. Everyone is not the same. Oh no, what a pain. Check out that frame. Did you catch his name? What can be gained when you live to defame? So, it's o.k. to be different, but always be tolerant {clement}

Opposites attract, diversity is attacked, prejudice is back, and I thought it never left because I feel singled out and all by myself.

This is not a phase. We are all actors on a stage. So stop trying to turn the page, and put and end to the rage. Just because it's not your scene, you don't have to be mean. You can't rewrite life's script. Stick in your bottom lip.

Opposites attract, diversity is attacked, prejudice is back, and I thought it never left because I feel singled out and all by myself

Galatians 6:2   Bear ye one another's burdens, and so fulfill the law of Christ

WEEK FOUR QUESTION THE WORK, NOT THE WORTH!

Titus3: 9 but avoid foolish questions, and genealogies, and contentions, and strivings about the law; for they are unprofitable and vain.

How many times have you been given a task and you have to shake your head and say what? All of a sudden you say, " Oops! Did I say that?" All owners know what needs to be done, but not all know what it takes. So, how do you as a worker bring balance to the force? Some of us will say, "I don't understand," or "It makes no sense," and my all time favorite, "That's a bad idea!" Who are you? Or better yet who made you judge, jury and executioner? How can you say it's a bad idea, and you've never done it before? Oh, I get it; it's not your idea, so that's why it doesn't count. Often, understanding will come quicker if we question the author and not the authenticity.

I remember taking a job at a convenience store where the cooler was always a mess. Every day I would come in to stock it up, clean it up, and throw the trash out. I was fine as long as no one questioned the way I worked. But then, I realized the boss spoke, and

I looked at him. I was in awe because he stopped looking at how it should be done, and proceeded to tell me how he wanted it done.

Luke 3:9 then he questioned with him in many words; but he answered him nothing.

I learned two things about getting things done through my owner. Number one: make a suggestion that seeks their approval (i.e. you think - if I do such and such will it be ok?) Number two: ask how to do it, not why you have to do it (i.e. how do you want me to set up the shelves?) If you do, by mistake, belittle someone's idea, just apologize and rephrase the question. This doesn't always work, but you never know until you try.

Sometimes, we don't understand, but there's nothing wrong with asking for understanding, instead of saying - it doesn't make sense. Of course it will not make sense, because you don't understand. So, ask for understanding. Say "I don't understand; can you simplify things for me?"

S.a.y. what you mean:

S - suggestions should seek their approval

A - ask how to do it

Y – yes, ask why also

Job 6:24 "teach me, and I will hold my tongue: and cause me to understand wherein I have erred"

ACTIVITY:

AN EXCUSE IS AN EXPLANATION , NOT A EXIT!

1. How many times has your excuse become your exit?

2. When will you be accountable for your reactions?

3. What will you do to be more responsible in the future?

4. Whom can you help apply this to his/her life?

Focus Thought:

Acts 28:23-24

"And when they had appointed him a day, there came many to him into [his] lodging; to whom he expounded and testified the kingdom of God, persuading them concerning Jesus, both out of the law of Moses, and [out of] the prophets, from morning till evening"
" And some believed the things which were spoken, and some believed not."

Coach's Corner

- The only time you should ask to be excused is when you're walking around someone, or when you're going to the bathroom.
- Stop trying to get by on an excuse
- An explanation should be more of a consultation, not a dissertation

---

80% of employers said they regularly conduct reference checks

-The Society for HR Mgt.

WEEK FIVE TRANSITIONAL LEADERSHIP

Accepting life's conditions without restriction

"It doesn't matter where you are, you are nowhere compared to where you can go." -Bob Proctor

Transition is a place, it's not a place of beginning or a place where your journey ends it's just a place where you end up at before you transcend into your true assignment. transition is all about timing today , tomorrow, soon, then , meanwhile , before, next week, as soon as , yesterday ,until & finally!

transition is the most informative part of your life that's when we're in the position to understand, this is the time were looking beyond the surface of the question , this is that moment when you realize 90% of the answers you seek are all around you just awaiting your 10% , just waiting for you to ask the right question! Transition isn't just a place it's also has a lot to do with your timing. sometimes transition is planned and often it's learned ; but when you realize it's about timing & location the adjustments get easier! Transition is the process of changing from one state or condition to another, Transition is a period of change, a metamorphosis, a conversion if i may . It is a time to let things go & hand things over and move unto your next assignment, Transition is your right of passage from poverty to prosperity, from conditions to permissions

transition in the hebrew is pronounced ma- ha- valve literally means passage

transition in the greek is pronounced ma-tau- va-cy

Human life is full of transition. There are different transitions in life. Transition involves movement, shift, change, relocation amongst other things. The transition might be moving from one country to another, changing jobs, getting married, promotion, starting new business, going to the mission field, God's call, going to a new school, pregnancy, terminal illness, retirement, divorce or anything that brings change from the normal routine.

Transition can be positive or negative. Positive transition usually involves promotion, greener pastures, marriage and any positive changes. Negative transition involves death, retirement, divorce and other negative changes.

Transition whether negative or positive sometimes brings feelings of anxiety, fear, apprehension, uncertainty, indecision, tension amongst other feelings."Nothing diminishes anxiety faster than action." -Walter Anderson These feelings can be very deep depending on how long one has been in the old status quo. Sometimes it depends on how rich the relationships were or how established, settled, rooted, happy one was in their former state.

Transition is that place of unfamiliar terrain ,it can be a scary and lonely place because God is transplanting you, your ministry ,your family & your job forward or backward. and you're steadily trying to transfer to a relationship that no longer serves you or the vision."Getting over a painful experience is much like crossing monkey bars. You have to let go at some point in order to move forward." -C.S. Lewis In transition there are ups and downs , ins and outs and turn abouts. you can't be stuck on tradition you won't endure the transition! Transition is not a down grade or an upgrade TRANSITION helps you to make the grade. I remember back when I was looking for a Job , people would ask me where are you working, I would answer i'M IN TRANSITION, people would ask me what do you do, I would answer i'm in TRANSITION , My answer should have been I'm in training because I was stuck between a dream and a job and if i would have adjusted my workflow to flow with my life i would have not been in transition for eleven months, see Transition is your transit to a better life . Transition is your personal transmission that your place in life is about the change. just a side note : Transition only becomes rough when you try to overturn person instead of turning over the position .That has become too much for you or it's not challenging enough so you underperform and over deliver, the problem is you need deliverance so the work you deliver is unacceptable! Let me explain there was a time in my life I didn't like where I lived because they didn't appreciate me & i Didn't appreciate them so anything i cooked and i'm pretty fat so i was a pretty good cook the issue is that my food was Nasty, I was burning stuff . when i moved from that situation i cooked and it was totally different. The season i was in at that point of my life affected the way I seasoned my food! you can't savor the flavor if you've lost the favor of the people

By changing nothing, nothing changes." -Tony Robbins - See more at:

5 keys of excellence for transition

Major life transitions -- moving to a new city, becoming a parent, retirement -- can be an exciting and invigorating part of life. Yet transitions, even happy ones, can also be stressful and bring up mixed feelings. Dr. Shannon **Kolakowski**

The best way to prepare for major transitions is to take some time for self-reflection. Use the following guide to help you to embrace change and make the most of your new role:

1.   **Recognize that transitions is your transmission to permission:**We naturally define ourselves in part by our surroundings. When these surrounds change, it can be disorienting. Getting married changes your identity from a single person to a partner. Having a child changes your sense of identity from wife or daughter to now include being a mother. A new job changes your identity or role at work. semone, for example, was delighted to have been giving a promotion at her company. Her new position had more responsibility, which she liked, but as a manager she no longer had the peer team she was used to working with. She missed her former colleagues and felt overwhelmed. She worried, *Am I really equipped for this job? Maybe I was better off before.* It took some time for her to re-build her sense of identity in her new role. As she became more comfortable in her new duties and with new colleagues, her work identity was reestablished.

2.   **Being in transition is a wonderful opportunity for growth without conditions.** Take a look at the parts of yourself and your life that you most value-- how can you bring those parts of yourself into your new role? Next, look at the areas of yourself that you'd like to make changes to. Perhaps you've been neglectful of some important area of your life. Transitions are an opportunity to begin practicing new habits and ways of interacting with others. For example, when Tracy got married to Heath, she used the wedding as a time to reflect on what kind of a partner she wanted to be and how she could work to make her marriage strong.

3.   **Transition feels strange when we won't accept the change**. In the midst of feeling a little lost during a transition, it can be easy to regret your decision. *Why did I break up with Dennis? I'm lonely and it's hard to find someone new*. When doubt creeps in, review the reasons you made your decision: *I broke up with Dennis because he didn't treat me very well and I wasn't happy in our relationship. I knew I didn't want to be with him long term, and wouldn't be able to move on while I was involved still with him.* When you see the big picture, it helps you move from feeling overwhelmed to understanding that this is a temporary adjustment, and while it's difficult now, you are willing to go through some uncertainty and discomfort for the long term gain.

4.   **Look at your life when you didn't allow self imposed restrictions to interfere with your transition.** What helped you get through that period in your life? Looking back, how do you feel about the past decisions you've made? What were you proud of, and what would you have done differently? Reflecting on your past can help you to make good decisions as you move forward.

5.   **When you're in transition changing the conditions shift the focus during transition.** One way to shift your focus is to look at others who may need your help. If you're at work, it may be a coworker who you notice is having a bad day. If you're in a prenatal yoga class, reach out to another mom-to-be that seems like she is having a hard time. Making an effort to support others helps you remember that everyone struggles at times, and that human connection can be a powerful aid in helping get through it.

Final thought

Let's face it; God's will is always changing us. He is always transforming us and molding us to be something different than we are. In the Word, God even refers to Himself as a potter and we are His clay. It's an easy image to see. A lump of clay is shaped into a vessel and then refined in the fire until it is becomes purified and hardened. Only then is worthy of use.

Change is never comfortable but it is a fact of life and it is the will of God. We are changed as we grow in age and maturity. We are changed when we accept Christ into our hearts. We are changed as we move deeper into a relationship with God and accept His will in our lives.

The bible is full of individuals, leaders and nations going through transition. There are invaluable lessons we can learn from the scriptures. Let's look at a few examples.

One of the hardest transitions one can make is moving from one's country, family and father's house to a foreign land. This is what Abraham did. "Now the LORD had said unto Abram, Get thee out of thy country, and from thy kindred, and from thy father's house, unto a land that I will shew thee:" Gen 12:1. When the transition is God initiated like Abraham's; God usually sends reassurance and promises as He did for Abraham; "And I will make of thee a great nation, and I will bless thee, and make thy name great; and thou shalt be a blessing: And I will bless them that bless thee, and curse him that curseth thee: and in thee shall all families of the earth be blessed." Gen 12:2-3. This reassurance and promise is usually very comforting and is medicine to the soul in dealing with the feelings of uncertainty and fear that creep in with the transition. God promise was that He would bless Abraham wherever he was going. My prayer for you is that God will bless you wherever you are going and in your new assignment! I encourage those in transition to seek God's mind on the matter in order to tap into His wisdom, comfort and counsel in the matter of transition. Sometimes going back home can also be difficult especially if one has been away for a long period of time.

Abraham did not resist transition but fully cooperated with God in the matter and He left us a rich legacy of faith, obedience and sacrifice that we should all emulate.

Ruth on the other hand lost her husband through sickness and was left lonely without a child after a decade of marriage. The death of a spouse can be one of the most traumatizing transitions one has to go through. Ruth was a Moabite married to a Hebrew. This was a mixed marriage. The God of the Hebrews was different from the Moabite god. Ruth's marriage was therefore a blended, cross cultural marriage. This kind of marriage is usually quite a transition. Ruth's husband left her in the prime of her womanhood without a child but she was not destitute. She had come to know the God of the Hebrew people and she was ready to entrust the rest of her life in His hands; "And Ruth said, entreat me not to leave thee, or to return from following after thee: for whither thou goest, I will go; and where thou lodgest, I will lodge: thy people shall be my people, and thy God my God: Where thou diest, will I die, and there will I be buried: the LORD do so to me, and more also, if ought but death part thee and me. When she saw that she was stedfastly minded to go with her, then she left speaking unto her." Ruth 1:16-18. There is hope for those going through traumatic transitions like Ruth. God blessed her super abundantly because she clung to Him during the time of transition. May the Lord help you to cling onto Him during whatever transition you are going through!

I can go on and on giving examples of people that went through transition in the Bible but I will stop here. I want to leave you with a few thoughts and scriptures that will help you during this time of transition;

1. Be open and flexible to God's plans, purposes and surprises in your new season. "For as the heavens are higher than the earth, so are my ways higher than your ways, and my thoughts than your thoughts." Isa 55:9

2. Surround yourself with Godly counsel in your new destination. "Without counsel purposes are disappointed: but in the multitude of counsellors they are established." Pro 15:22

3. Be slow to speak, quick to listen and extremely alert in your new assignment. "Wherefore, my beloved brethren, let every man be swift to hear, slow to speak, slow to wrath:" Jam 1:19

4. Look for a Christ-centered, Bible-believing, Spirit-filled and lively Church. Deepen your relationship with God by being committed there. It is a safe haven. "Not forsaking the assembling of ourselves together, as the manner of some is; but exhorting one another: and so much the more, as ye see the day approaching. For if we sin wilfully after that we have received the knowledge of the truth, there remaineth no more sacrifice for sins, But a certain fearful looking for of judgment and fiery indignation, which shall devour the adversaries." Heb 10:25-27

5. Learn from your past mistakes and start a new leaf of life in your new destination. "Remember ye not the former things, neither consider the things of old. Behold, I will do a new thing; now it shall spring forth; shall ye not know it? I will even make a way in the wilderness, and rivers in the desert." Isa 43:18-19 "For I know the thoughts that I think toward you, saith the LORD, thoughts of peace, and not of evil, to give you an expected end." Jer 29:11

6. Do not entertain feelings of fear and uncertainty. Confess God's Word over your life. "Fear thou not; for I am with thee: be not dismayed; for I am thy God: I will strengthen thee; yea, I will help thee; yea, I will uphold thee with the right hand of my righteousness." Isa 41:10

7. Write down what you want to achieve in your new destination and ask your Pastor to pray with you about these projections. " Commit thy way unto the LORD; trust also in him; and he shall bring it to pass. " Psa 37:5 "And the LORD answered me, and said, Write the vision, and make it plain upon tables, that he may run that readeth it. For the vision is yet for an appointed time, but at the end it shall speak, and not lie: though it tarry, wait for it; because it will surely come, it will not tarry. Hab 2:2-3

WEEK SIX LOOKING THE PART

It's hard to look the part, when your confidence is fractured. it's hard to look the part when all around you is falling apart. It's hard to look the part when you're suffering because of a broken heart.I remember when I lost my job I was diligently looking, but I couldn't find anything I began to question my skills, I begin to question God. what do you do between jobs And I thought it was hard when I was dying for a paycheck and living for a bill! you can't begin to understand What it feels like, To be in survival mode you're close, your shoes your undergarments thrift store bought. every 2 months you need a new pair of shoes. I was wearing the same clothes take him to the cleaners not realizing that your body sheds everyday is so You become so accustomed to the stink you don't even blink. "Don't be looking for a part until you look the part"

"You can't dress for the job; you have to get the career you want"
I Samuel 16:7   But the LORD said unto Samuel, Look not on his countenance, or on the height of his stature; because I have refused him: for [the LORD seeth] not as man seeth; for man looketh on the outward appearance, but the LORD looketh on the heart.

"Your composition can be determine by your disposition"
II Corinthians 5:12   For we commend not ourselves again unto you, but give you occasion to glory on our behalf, that ye may have somewhat to [answer] them which glory in appearance, and not in heart.

Why reinvent the wheel?
Hebrews 6:12   That ye be not slothful, but followers of them who through faith and patience inherit the promises.

Dress up and look your best.
Ecclesiastes 9:8   Let thy garments be always white; and let thy head lack no ointment.

Wash your face and comb your hair.
Mathew 6:17   But thou, when thou fastest, anoint thine head, and wash thy face;

Focus Thought:

Real People do Real things And if you have to question yourself then it's not Real just practice – Robert T. Lester

Coach's Corner

- **Often when people have a job to do, their style of dress reflects their work. You will never reach the palace working like a peasant. Never forget: a job is what you do, not who you are.**
- **You won't look like a winner until you feel like one. Looking the part is not just cosmetic; it is a character building experience as well.**
- You can't end up a winner ; if you begin whining first!

Your telephone conversation could last 10 minutes to an hour with the hiring manager

–Wall Street Journal

Focus Thought:

Thessalonians 5:14

"Now we exhort
you, brethren, warn them that are unruly, comfort the
feebleminded, support the weak, be patient toward all [men]."
Coach's Corner

- Take your time and do things right.
- Everyone gets frustrated. The challenge is
  not to frustrate others.
- Treat others how you wish to be treated
- A fine is a tax for doing wrong ;a tax is a fine for doing
  well

86% of executives said cover letters are

important when evaluating job candidates –

National Association of Workforce

Development, Professionals

WEEK SEVEN MONKEY SEE, MONKEY DO!

So many of us talk a great game, but we are awful players. Someone is always going to be watching you, and just when you think they can't do it like you, they not only do it; they do it better. Some of us love to play dirty, but don't want to get dirty.

Luke 6:31 "And as ye would that men should do to you, do ye also to them likewise."

How many times have you heard do as I say, not as I do? Have you ever considered that the reason people are not doing what you say, is because of what you do!

James 1:22-24 But be ye doers of the word, and not hearers only, deceiving your own selves.

For if any be a hearer of the word, and not a doer, he is like unto a man beholding his natural face in a glass:

For he beholdeth himself, and goeth his way, and straightway forgetteth what manner of man he was.

If you do not honor your words, why should anyone else? Look, I only want to say this once: people will constantly do what they see, because it looks easier than following the instructions. This meditation can also be used at work, so your words and your heart become one.

Psalms 19:14 Let the words of my mouth, and the meditation of my heart, be acceptable in thy sight, O LORD, my strength, and my redeemer.

When people don't do what they say, in the bible, it's considered "double-minded," and in the workforce a double standard. Either way, it's the quickest way to double your trouble. If you will not lead by setting the right example, the league will definitely follow the wrong example! Always remember: do what you say, also when you're training others. *"The example you set is often the sample that's produced."*

~ *Michael Gatewood*

Mathew 6:18   that thou appear not unto men to fast, but unto thy Father which is in secret: and thy Father, which seeth in secret, shall reward thee openly.

ACTIVITY:

" [R-D/A+ I= F] Reacting out of desperation instead of Acting on inspiration equals frustration"

1.   How many problems have you created today?

2.   What can you do to be more patient?

3.   Is it safe to say that the reason you're in trouble is because you didn't seek help when needed?

4.   What will you do differently?

Always be Confidential

It has been duly noted that silence can't be misquoted, but pointless conversation has brought about great devastation.

Instead of repeating what you hear, you should hold that information dear, because if telling is a must, you'll never gain anyone's trust. "He said/she said has rendered many dead." Why not keep it to yourself and promote better health. You must praise in the public and critique in private. Then if things go awry, the friendship won't go bye-bye.

It has been duly noted that silence can't be misquoted, but pointless conversation has brought about great devastation.

Speaking out of turn could get someone burned. The story is all changed and the blame is on your name. Your head is tilted in shame. Your character is in flames. Now, you wish you were silent. That's not what you meant. Silence is the golden rule, but sometimes you feel yellow. Life will teach you when to settle, and the Spirit will teach you when to meddle.

It has been duly noted that silence can't be misquoted, but pointless conversation has brought about great devastation.

Philippians 2:14 -15 Do all things without murmurings and disputing: That ye may be blameless and harmless, the sons of God, without rebuke, in the midst of a crooked and perverse nation, among whom ye shine as lights in the world

Mathew 6:18   that thou appear not unto men to fast, but unto thy Father which is in secret: and thy Father, which seeth in secret, shall reward thee openly.

WEEK EIGHT WHAT TIME IS IT?

Generally, there are eight to ten hours in a shift. The reason I say this is because we pour so much of ourselves into our work, that when we get home we have nothing left. You have spent a lot of time with this company, but how much time have they invested in you? If the money you're paid is not enough to make you part owner, consider your purpose.

Psalm 90:12 so teach [us] to number our days, that we may apply [our] hearts unto wisdom.
The first key to being a dedicated employee is the quality of work you do within your limits. The second key is the quantity of the work you do within your limits. Owners don't concern themselves with the hours you take to do a job. They look at the job you do with the hours you were given.

We need to stop visiting our home and living at work. Go home, and then you'll know where your child is, because you'll be at home with him. Many kids receive life experience credit before they enter college instead of the parenting they needed when they were home. Do I need to say more? Am I hitting home? Because that's where I'm trying to take you. In the words of Carl Winslow, "Go home, go home, and go home." The reality is - Family Matters. Never be more than fifteen minutes early, unless specifically asked. Even then, you can still say no; your time is valuable. They will treasure that if you remember this one rule and apply it - less is more. We've all heard the old adage - "The early bird catches the worm." I'm sorry you haven't made it to the blue-collar workforce. The new adage is - "The early bird becomes the worm." Owners appreciate when you're early sometimes, because you've given more time to them than yourself, but more than 15 minutes puts more time in their hands, which creates busy work for your hands.

Ephesians 5:15-16 See then that ye walk circumspectly, not as fools, but as wise, redeeming the time, because the days are evil.

It's time you make the most of your time, and schedule it around you. Don't let them schedule during family time. Remember: eight hours belong to them; sixteen belong to you. You're in control. Request your days off. Stop working all the overtime. Most of the time, after twenty hours of overtime, you're working for the company and the state. Why are you working off the clock? Does your family know the reason you don't have money is that you're not clocking in? If you're on a job, and they ask why you stayed late, or why you left early, it's because they're on a budget. The more time you spend at work, the more it costs the company. If you cost more than you produce, it's all a matter of time before your time is up. It all comes down to this - Time is Money.

ACTIVITY:

"If you're busy counting the reasons why you can't, you'll never see the reason why you can."

1. How many reasons can you find to get out of work?

2. How would you feel if this happened to you?

3. On a scale of one to ten, how do you rate your job - terrible or
    terrific?

4. How many reasons can you find to go to work?

Always be cognitive

To think out loud, doesn't mean you're in the clouds
To think on your feet, doesn't mean you will suffer defeat
To think under stress, doesn't mean you're the best
To think not at all is where most of us fall

We all have moments of regret and times of deliberation, but it's not the end of the celebration. It's hard making a decision when things aren't in tact; you can't think of everything that's a well-known fact. It's good to think ahead, with tragedy lurking in every hedge. Just keep a level head. Information is everyone's ally, so network. It's not only up to you. If you can't see another's point of view, how will they see you?

To think out loud, doesn't mean you're in the clouds
To think on your feet, doesn't mean you will suffer defeat
To think under stress, doesn't mean you're the best
To think not at all is where most of us fall

Don't beat yourself up or praise your name too early, because if you didn't achieve it as a team no one is truly worthy. People who do not think often speak too soon, and then before you know it understanding has left the room. Some people say my body doesn't wake until noon. News flash it starts in the womb. If you share what you know, it's not a hard workflow.

To think out loud, doesn't mean you're in the clouds
To think on your feet, doesn't mean you will suffer defeat
To think under stress, doesn't mean you're the best
To think not at all is where most of us fall

Ecclesiastes 8:5-6 whoso keepeth the commandment shall feel no evil thing: and a wise man's heart discerneth both time and judgment.
Because to every purpose there is time and judgment, therefore the misery of man [is] great upon him.

WEEK NINE PROMOTIONS COME FROM WITH IN

You ever wonder why you can't get to the next level? Four songs come to mind: "You talk too much and you never shut up!" Don't loud talk the owner. Hold your tongue before you say something they never forget and you regret. The second song is: "You can take this job and shove it. I ain't working here no more!" If that's your mind state, your family will soon be in the state of an emergency, because you'll have no job. The third song (supervisors' all-time favorite): "What have you done for me lately?" O.k. you busted your hump last week. What about today? You see, striving for excellence is a daily task not a one-time event, and the fourth is my favorite - "Lean with it rock with it!" Go with the flow; quit standing out, and just be outstanding.

Are you taking initiatives to do things without someone holding your hand? Are you showing your teammates the work or complaining about how they work? Be an effective worker, not an effective busy body; be one who is busy, not one who just looks busy. Do you have a friendly disposition?

Proverbs 5:13-14
A merry heart maketh a cheerful countenance: but by sorrow of the heart the spirit is broken.
The heart of him that hath understanding seeketh knowledge: but the mouth of fools feedeth on foolishness.

Can people talk to you about what needs to be done, and you respond to what needs to be done rather than react to how heavy the load is. What does this have to do with promotion? It has everything to do with promotion. Let me tell you a little secret. You must ask yourself - Am I worthy of promotion? If the answer is yes, know this: the power of promotion comes from you. How so? Stop looking at the problem and look for the solution. People are tired of lipservice. If you get into the habit of promoting better work ethics, people will get in the habit of promoting you. Remember: the power is yours to command, control, and/or condemn.

Proverbs 27:1-2
Boast not thyself of to morrow; for thou knowest not what a day may bring forth.
Let another man praise thee, and not thine own mouth; a stranger, and not thine own lips.

ACTIVITY:

"If it doesn't make cents, maybe it's nonsense"

1. Do you read all the instructions?

2. How many shortcuts have you taken?

3. Have shortcuts ever made it hard for everyone around you?

4. What will you do differently to support the team?

Focus Thought:

Proverbs 16:25
"There is a way that seemeth right unto a man, but the end thereof [are] the ways of death"
Acts 28:27
"For the heart of this people is waxed gross, and their ears are dull of hearing, and their eyes have they closed; lest they should see with [their] eyes, and hear with [their] ears, and understand with [their] heart, and should be converted, and I should heal them."

Coach's Corner

- How often do you read the fine print?
- Are you committed to this conversation in heart?
- Shortcuts are the quickest way to cut away from people. Take your time and do things right.

- Stupid is what stupid does, so ask more questions.
- The quickest way to loose a job is to loose interest

75% of hiring managers said they prefer a chronological resume that lists your most recent job first – Career Journal

Always be careful

A person who is careful will not be careless
They take their time to prevent any mess. Their decisions are informed
and the outcome above the norm.

No need to worry or be in a hurry; you've checked everything twice.
It'll turn out nice. Don't wait too long; something might go wrong.

A person who is careful will not be careless
They take their time to prevent any mess. Their decisions are informed
and the outcome above the norm.

A person who is careful can be very meticulous; people who are careless
find this ridiculous. You never have to contemplate because you always
anticipate. You will make mistakes before it's all said and done, but because
you were careful you still would have won.

A person who is careful will not be careless.
They take their time to prevent any mess their decisions are informed
and the outcome above the norm.

*Ecclesiastes 3:22 wherefore I perceive that [there is] nothing better, than that a man
should rejoice in his own works; for that [is] his portion: for who shall bring him to see
what shall be after him?*

ACTIVITY:

"You will never reach the finish line, if you do not approach the starting line"

1. What is your definition of a loser?

2. What is worse than a looser?

    Someone who hasn't even begun

3. What's holding you back from winning your race?

4. What will you do to finish your race?

Always be competent

When you know who you are and know your ability, this builds competence and stability

Experience comes from longevity
Complete skills are a necessity
Endurance is a quality
Coaching is a big commodity
Now you have the recipe; go develop your ability

When you know who you are and know your ability, this builds competence and stability

Who you are depends on what you read
What you are is often determined by your speech
Who you are is determined by what you need
Where you go depends on what you seek
What you find is determined in your mind
Now, you have all the ingredients. I hope right now you're competent

When you know who you are and know your ability, this builds competence and stability

1 Corinthians 4:1 let a man so account of us, as of the ministers of Christ, and stewards of the mysteries of God.
4:2 Moreover it is required in stewards, that a man be found faithful.

WEEK TEN HOW TO SURVIVE C.C.E.

A Constantly Changing Environment

Before you write the job off, you must see everything it has to offer. My ex-wife has been on her job for 25 years. I asked her - how did you do it? She said, "I just had to be flexible and realize this too shall pass." She would look for innovative ways to pump up the volume at work. She would sing most of her shift to make the day go by, and she changed positions every five years, which increased her knowledge of the company. It also made her an asset within the company. So you see, sometimes the more you know, the more empowered you are to do more for the company and for yourself. Her attitude and approach also separates a worker from the people going nowhere fast.

My pastor would say, "Smile, so people know you're not ugly; you're just looking that way!" Just joking - eh ah ha! Change position, so you don't fill like the career is not going anywhere. A change in position is like a breath of fresh air. Just changing your disposition only pollutes the air. Challenge yourself to try something new, instead of creating a challenge to resist change.

"People generally say the grass is greener on the other side, only because their eyes are still closed, and they're just green with envy."

Ecclesiastes
   3:1   to every [thing there is] a season, and a time to every purpose under the heaven:
   3:2   A time to be born, and a time to die; a time to plant, and a time to pluck up [that which is] planted;
   3:3   a time to kill, and a time to heal; a time to break down, and a time to build up;
   3:4   A time to weep, and a time to laugh; a time to mourn, and a time to dance;
   3:5   A time to cast away stones, and a time to gather stones together; a time to embrace, and a time to refrain from embracing;
   3:6   a time to get, and a time to lose; a time to keep, and a time to cast away;
   3:7   a time to rend, and a time to sew; a time to keep silence, and a time to speak;
   3:8   a time to love, and a time to hate; a time of war, and a time of peace.
Times are never ending and always changing, what ever it is, you will not survive if you're not flexible

WEEK ELLEVEN GIVE ME A BREAK!

Don't you get tired of working a lot of hours without a break? You ever blow up because someone interrupts your thought process or your work in progress? Have you ever felt like you deserve a break, but were afraid to ask? I remember a time when I couldn't afford to take a break; do you? Well, surprise! Surprise! We are going to take paid breaks; sounds good doesn't it?

Here's how you know. When you normally get mad because of an interruption, don't get mad; just help those who ask of you and enjoy your break. You know that meeting you have to go to? Don't spend a few extra minutes more at work because you'll just cut in to your break!

You're probably saying - what are you talking about? I'm telling you that a break means to separate into parts, according to Webster. Now, the next time you get interrupted, be happy and remember you're on break.

Mathew 11:28
Come unto me, all [ye] that labour and are heavy laden, and I will give you rest.
Interruptions, meetings, and change in assignments should be considered a break, but if you can't see it; you want believe it.

Mathew 9:28-29
9:28   and when he was come into the house, the blind men came to him: and Jesus saith unto them, Believe ye that I am able to do this? They said unto him, Yea, Lord. 9:29   then touched he their eyes, saying, According to your faith be it unto you.

ACTIVITY:

"It's okay to make an error; just don't be in error"

1. Do you remember when you were as wrong as two left shoes?
What happened?

2. Was it easy to admit your mistake?

3. How many have you scolded for a mistake?

Focus Thought:

James 5:16

"Confess [your] faults one to another, and pray one for another, that ye may be healed. The effectual fervent prayer of a righteous man availeth much."

.
Coach's Corner

- Two wrongs don't make a right.
- Two rights don't make a left.
- If you want to stay in business, mind your business.

- Admitting fault is a duty, not a
  PRIVELEDGE!!

On average, there are 4.2 Job hunters for every job opening –U.S. Bureau of Labor Statistics

Focus Thought:

GEM

"Benefits are beneficial when you realize It's not that there are doing to little ,it is you who is not doing enough."

. Coach's Corner
- We all are tempted by something.
- Often times, the power to becoming temperate is in going through our own temptation.
- The same will you use to be tempted is the same energy you can use to overcome.
- Ability is good but stability is better

www.Ahajokes.com

19% of the labor force works for big businesses (500 employees or more) -USBLS

Always believe in cooperation

Always believe in cooperation. This strategy can build a nation whereas conflict can create hesitation and separation

There will be times when the work is up to you and there are challenging odds in everything you do. Payday is the day everyone wants to play; it's also the day some get lost along the way.

Always believe in cooperation. This strategy can build a nation whereas conflict can create hesitation and separation

Sometimes no one wants to listen, and sometimes, when you can't speak, you must keep a steady pace; do not accept defeat. Remember - cooperation can build a team, when conflict just builds steam. Sometimes, you'll be behind. It's hard to be in a bind if you depend on your team all the time. It's not about you when things are just right, and it's not about them when things are completely wrong. You can remain a team if you just get along.

Always believe in cooperation. This strategy can build a nation whereas conflict can create hesitation and separation

Amos 3:3   Can two walk together, except they agree?

WEEK TWELVE IT ALL STARTED AFTER I CLOCKED IN!

Today, I just don't feel like being here. I would like a little time off. So, I press on, and then I meet a lady who was laid off from work. She said she couldn't find a job for eight months. Can you imagine how depressed she was? It figures; can't live with a job; can't live without one. Well, so much for feeling lackadaisical. Let's face it; the only reason you *feel there is nothing to do is because you're doing nothing*.

This is probably a hard concept for you, but you need to know. *Money doesn't make the world go around, but money does make the bills go down*. So, stop being lackadaisical and be grateful you have a job that pays you a decent wage with great benefits. Also, if you find something to do, you are creating job security. If the owners could do it by themselves, do you think you would be clocking in? Probably not. If you don't believe you're receiving a decent wage with benefits, then you don't know that it's a privilege, not a right.

James 4:2
"Ye lust, and have not: ye kill, and desire to have, and cannot obtain: ye fight and war, yet ye have not, because ye ask not."

Sometimes, you just can't ask for what you want; you have to sell yourself. Point out your talents that will benefit the company. A lot of times, companies don't take an interest in you because you've taken no interest in their points of view. Now that you've learned to be specific when you sell yourself, if what they offer is not what you want, then don't sell out and accept it. No offer is above negotiation unless you say no. There are going to be times when the offer won't change. If you've received their best offer, take it for now. But let them know that you are looking to advance, because your responsibility is bigger than you; you have family to take care of.

2 Thessalonians 3:10
"For even when we were with you, this we commanded you, that if any would not work, neither should he eat."

There are times we all would like to do better things. My advice for you is to press on, because *you want feel the pressure of being at a dead end if you're pressing in to begin.*

ACTIVITY:

Don't be tempted by all; be temperate in all

1. Have you ever been tempted to say what's on your mind?

2. What do you do to resist temptation?

3. Was it easy for you to convince others to be temperate?

4. What does lackadaisical mean?

WEEK THIRTEEN CALLING OFF VS CALLING IN

I don't feel good. My baby is sick. I don't have a ride. My car broke down. My _____ died. My_____ is in the hospital. My clothes are dirty. I miss the bus, and my all-time favorite - I'm having personal problems. I'm sure I missed some reasons you have called off. Hey, sometimes these excuse are valid, but does it justify you calling off? Let me ask a few questions:

- Are your debts high?
- Do you have a full-time or part-time schedule?
- How many hours in a week have you called off?
- How many times have you called in to say - I'm going to be late?
- Do you notice your hours being cut from week to week?
- WHEN YOU REQUEST DAYS OFF, DO YOU GET THEM?

My point here is this: the reason you're not making any money could be that you take too much time off. Unless you get sick time, vacation time, and overtime, it's time you call in some favors to see if people will help you out so you can stay at work. Some people call off because they're sick of working. Remember: every time you call off, you're taking away from someone else's time off. Everyone gets tired of the work, but that's the time you need to find a career, so you can leave that dead-end job. Leaving a job should be a process not a problem. Here is how:

- Always go on the hunt first
- Notify your job that you are looking to better yourself
- Ask if they can give you a reference
- Once you are hired, give two weeks notice
- Do your best to leave on good terms

Remember how you leave a job is how you'll begin your career, so be positive. I hope the next time you call in is to see if you are needed.

2 Corinthians 9:6-8

" *But this [I say], He which soweth sparingly shall reap also sparingly; and he which soweth bountifully shall reap also bountifully. Every man according as he purposeth in his heart, [so let him give]; not grudgingly, or of necessity: for God loveth a cheerful giver. And God [is] able to make all grace abound toward you; that ye, always having all sufficiency in all [things], may abound to every good work":*

Please give more of your time, because the more you give of yourself, the more things will be given to you.

ACTIVITY:

"It ave to be nice; it Co$t to be nasty"

1. Do you remember when you paid the price for foolishness?

2. Do you think you would go another route with what you know now, and why?

3. How will you apply this principle daily?

Focus Thought:

"Be ye angry, and sin not: let not the sun go down upon your wrath."

Ephesians 4:26
. Coach's Corner

- Your good deeds, your misdeeds - these are all
  returned to you.
- Opportunity always knocks at the least opportune moment.
- It's hard doing good to those who hurt you. Just remember - only good deeds go unpunished.

26% of the labor force works for med. Size

business –USBLS (100-499employees)

Always believe in keeping your composure

If you don't want too much exposure you will watch your composure. Your every reaction and satisfaction is revealed on your face, so please don't become displaced or you will lose sight of grace.

When things are in error, you need to be thankful in this era, and life will be filled with great measure, pressed down and shaken together.

When things go right, be loose with your blessing. The truth of your confession can save a soul from life's lesson.

It's ok when things don't go your way; always remember your success and never settle for anything less.

If you don't want too much exposure, you will watch your composure. Your every reaction and satisfaction is revealed on your face, so please don't become displaced, or you will lose sight of grace.

When people call you out, know what you're all about, and you'll never fall out
Don't be subject to abuse for rudeness or the truth. Seek peace and make a truce.

Always do what's right and you'll never be uptight
Don't subject your body to stress and you'll receive the proper rest.

If you don't want too much exposure you will watch your composure. Your every reaction and satisfaction is revealed on your face, so please don't become displaced or you will lose sight of grace.

Proverbs 27:19 as in water face [answereth] to face, so the heart of man to man.

WEEK FOURTEEN DON'T WORRY BE HAPPY

I say that because it's hard to smile when a supervisor has berated you. It feels like you get the dirty work, because you do. Sometimes when they come to work, they bring their dirty laundry with them and expect you to handle their problems. The only thing is that you have work issues pending. These kind of people bend whichever way the wind blows. You try to do your best and they just angry I'm sure you've heard misery loves company. Well, anxiety loves you and now your worried because you don't know what to do.

Isaiah 3:10 Say ye to the righteous, that [it shall be] well [with him]: for they shall eat the fruit of their doings.

No matter what happens, do what's right; people are known for what they do. I know it's hard, but if you can't respect the person, then at least respect the position that they hold.

Colossians 3:22 Servants, obey in all things [your] masters according to the flesh; not with eye service, as men pleasers; but in singleness of heart, fearing God.

Remember: this is where you work, and the reason you're angry is because you're taking it personally. Work is where you are personable. This means no more eye service; just do it and get her done!

Romans 14:5 one man esteemeth one day above another: another esteemeth every day [alike]. Let every man be fully persuaded in his own mind.

Did you know that when you get angry the seritonin and neoepinephrine in your brain becomes active, and the more you use these chemicals, the harder it is to concentrate?

Not only do you lose concentration, but it's also hard to remember too.

Acts 24:25 And as he reasoned of righteousness, temperance, and judgment to come, Felix trembled, and answered, Go thy way for this time; when I have a convenient season, I will call for thee.

Sometimes when we're angry, we tend to put things off. We need to quit putting things off, because most times when **you put things off, they fall on others**.

ACTIVITY:

"If you stay ready, you don't have to get ready"

1. Do you have any goals in life?

2. Are you applying them to your life?

3. What's stopping you?

4. Now that you've identified the enemy of your success, are you ready to attack and when?

Focus Thought:

Colossians 3:22-23

"Servants, obey in all things [your] masters according to the flesh; not with eye service, as men pleasers; but in singleness of heart, fearing God"
"And whatsoever ye do, do [it] heartily, as to the Lord, and not unto men.
Coach's Corner

- It's amazing how many reasons we can find not to work, but then we complain about money.
- Service with a smile? Oh, I'm sorry it's not pay day yet.
- Job wanted making more dough…try a bakery!

80% of all job openings are not advertised. Since friends of employees and other insiders usually fill these unadvertised job openings, they are often referred as the "hidden Job market"-CNN Money, Workforce Management

Focus Thought:

II Timothy 4:2-7

4:2 Preach the word; be instant in season, out of season; reprove, rebuke, exhort with all longsuffering and doctrine.

4:3 For the time will come when they will not endure sound doctrine; but after their own lusts shall they heap to themselves teachers, having itching ears;

4:4 And they shall turn away [their] ears from the truth, and shall be turned unto fables.

4:5 But watch thou in all things, endure afflictions, do the work of an evangelist, make full proof of thy ministry.

4:6 For I am now ready to be offered, and the time of my departure is at hand.

4:7 I have fought a good fight, I have finished [my] course, I have kept the faith:

. Coach's Corner

- "Failing to plan is planning to fail." Effie Jones

- **Who are you?**
  One who makes things happen?
  One who watches things happen?
  Or one who wonders what happened?

55% of the labor force works for small businesses- USBLS (under 100 employees)

Always be cool

Always be cool; don't act a fool. This is the reason you must follow the rules, and if you still don't see, let me take you to school.

What do you do when someone's picking on you? Why fight back and be plowed off the track? Why make a point and still be wrong? Don't go along to get along and then moan and groan? Don't want to get where you belong?

Always be cool; don't act a fool. This is the reason you must follow the rules, and if you still don't see, let me take you to school.

Don't be sold out; just hold out. Eventually, they will sell out, being cool with the rules is what it's all about. Rules set limits and guidelines you can reach, but we can't make exceptions if were going to teach. You can win in the fix you're in; just follow the rules. It's called discipline.

Always be cool; don't act a fool. This is the reason you must follow the rules, and if you still don't see, let me take you to school.

2 Timothy 2:5   and if a man also strives for masteries, [yet] is he not crowned, except he strives lawfully?

WEEK FIFTEEN TOO MUCH FOR TO LITTLE

They want me to clean the restrooms, clean the windows, sweep and mop the floor, sweep the parking lot, empty the trash, clean the vents, stock the cooler, smile and greet the guests, and order groceries, not necessarily in that order, and all they're paying me is minimum wage. I think it's amazing how we get mad about work at work. We don't like the wage we're paid, but when we were hired, we still accepted the job with low wages and all. You could have refused, but you didn't. Some of us are so grateful to have a job that we don't inquire about the wage until payday. Let me let you in on a secret - it's hard to get people to pay you for your work ethics, but not impossible. In most businesses, you will always have more work than people, because the more people you have the less profit you make.

I've never understood why when you have less people, more work gets done, but then I realized. The less you make responsible for certain tasks, the more accountable people become. {There's no one to blame} Some people decide that since the pay is less, that's how much work they will do. Oh, ye of little faith - Luke 16:10 - He that is faithful in that which is least is faithful also in much: and he that is unjust in the least is unjust also in much. There are times when the wage is less, but the hours are more (you know, overtime)

If you want a better wage, ask a better question:
- What do you pay someone with my experience?
- What do you pay someone in this position?

Sometimes there will be people with more experience than you. Even so, sometimes *will* outweighs *skill*. Take a few minutes and list what makes you an asset and not a liability.

And remember James 4:2-3 ye lust, and have not: ye kill, and desire to have, and cannot obtain: ye fight and war; yet ye have not, because ye ask not.
Ye ask, and receive not, because ye ask amiss, that ye may consume [it] upon your lusts.
You'll ***never face disappointment if you are specific in your appointment.*** If the money still isn't right, ask what you have to accomplish to receive a pay increase. Don't get upset with the answer; remember, you asked the question.

"Let every man abide in the same calling wherein he was called" I Corinthians 7:20

Always be cheerful

Always be cheerful because it costs too much to be miserable

Be cheerful when debts are high

Be cheerful when there is no cloud in the sky

Be cheerful when esteem is low

Be cheerful for the things that don't last

Be cheerful when you just don't know

Be cheerful when treated as an outcast

Be cheerful when the body is weak

Be cheerful when folks will not speak

Be cheerful when life becomes stress

Be cheerful cleaning up someone else's mess

Be cheerful because anything else would be foolishness

Always be cheerful because it costs too much to be miserable

Mathew 14:27   But straightway Jesus spake unto them, saying, be of good cheer; it is I; be not afraid.

ACTIVITY:

"A good name is more precious than any gain"

1. **What do people call you?**

2. **Have you ever been called out of your name?**

3. **When people here your name, do you sense satisfaction?**

4. **Do you like your name? Why or why not?**

5. **What will you answer to?**

Focus Thought:

Ecclesiastes 7:1

" A good name [is] better than precious ointment; and the day of death than the day of one's birth."
. Coach's Corner

- **It's not what they call you, but it's what you answer to.**
~Tyler Perry

The Standard Occupational Classification System includes over 840 separate occupations in the United States –U.S. Department of labor

---

CHAPTER THREE EMPLOYMENT MATTERS

What do people want from their job?

Abraham Maslow's Factory Survey
Rate the ten items below from one to ten according to what you believe people want from
their job, with one being what people want most and ten being what people want least from their job.

Reasons	My Ranking	Survey Ranking
Full appreciation of work being done.		
Feeling part of a team		
Help with personal problems		
Job Security		
High Salary		
Interesting Work		
Company Promotion		
A devoted supervisor		
Good working conditions		
Soft Skills		

This survey is listed in the order of importance, according to Maslow's research.

As you go through this book, you will realize that promotions come from within. Job security comes from overcoming your insecurities within you. The reason your work is not appreciated is because you don't appreciate the work. Last but not least, the reason the work is not interesting, is because you haven't taken an interest in the work. This book is designed to help you recommit to the work you are doing, and prepare you to go from a job to a career.

7 Reasons we're better off working

Self-confidence or self-worth

1. I Timothy 5:8, 18

But if any provide not for his own, and especially for those of his own house, he hath denied the faith, and is worse than an infidel.
For the scripture saith, Thou shalt not muzzle the ox that treadeth out the corn. And, The labourer [is] worthy of his reward.

Time Management

2. Psalms 90:12

So teach [us] to number our days, that we may apply [our] hearts unto wisdom

Submission & Authority

3. Hebrews 13:17

Obey them that have the rule over you, and submit yourselves: for they watch for your souls, as they that must give account, that they may do it with joy, and not with grief: for that [is] unprofitable for you.

Forgiveness

4. Proverbs 3:3-4

3:3 Let not mercy and truth forsake thee: bind them about thy neck; write them upon the table of thine heart:

   3:4 So shalt thou find favour and good understanding in the sight of God and man.

Team Work

5. Philippians 2:4

Look not every man on his own things, but every man also on the things of others.

[P.E.] Patience & Endurance

6. Galatians 6:9

And let us not be weary in well doing: for in due season we shall reap, if we faint not.

Effective Communication

7. Proverbs 16:21

The wise in heart shall be called prudent: and the sweetness of the lips increaseth learning.

Matthew 18:19

Again I say unto you, that if two of you shall agree on earth as touching anything that they shall ask, it shall be done for them of my Father, which is in heaven.

AGREEMENT

We, your coaches, agree to instruct you in positive job search techniques in a clear and precise manner. We will provide an environment that will help you locate your own job and will empower you to become self-sufficient.

We will provide you with the tools necessary for you to succeed (pencils, pens, paper, & workshops) until you are able to do so for yourself.

We will respect and treat you as the intelligent adult men and women that you are.

Team Coach_____

Date _____

I, your team player, agree to treat this workshop as I would a job. I will be on time every day and will reschedule other personal business, which would conflict with the workshop. If I am more than (7) minutes late, I will call out for consideration of other members, and stay later for my tardiness. I will approach each session with an open mind, and a positive attitude. I will dress appropriately (within my means) for each session or interview. I agree to be an active player on the team during this workshop. I agree to an active job search until I achieve employment and or become self-sufficient. I understand that there is a handbook that must be followed, and that violation of this agreement may force my discharge from the workshop for the morale of others.

Team Player_____

Date_____

WHY DO PEOPLE QUIT, EXCERPT FROM FORBES WEBSITE

WRITTEN BY ALAN HALL

He recently discovered an alarming fact—even in a climate of business uncertainty and an unemployment rate of 7.8 percent, more than 2 million Americans are voluntarily leaving their jobs every month. The U.S. Department of Labor Bureau of Labor Statistics calls the category "Quits." While the percentage of overall turnover has remained relatively steady at approximately 1.69 percent per month over the past decade, the number of voluntary "quits" is continuing to grow and will not be decreasing anytime soon, according to the bureau.

Even in a down economy 2 million Americans quit their job every month.

Why are so many people quitting? A report from Grow America compiled research from several sources. In truth, the majority of people, quitting or not, are currently unhappy in their corporate jobs. A study by Harris Interactive indicates a full 74 percent of people would today consider finding a new job. The most recent Mercer's What's Working study says 32 percent are actively looking. The reasons for their unhappiness:

A recent study by Accenture reports:

1) They don't like their boss (31%),
2) A lack of empowerment (31%),
3) Internal politics (35%) and
4) Lack of recognition (43%).

Many cite the desire to become their own boss. A Business Insider survey of 225 executives reports 22 percent want to launch their own companies. Why are they willing to make the sacrifice and take the risk? They want to run an enterprise their way. Deep in their hearts, they feel and know they will enjoy more satisfaction and fulfillment by establishing a healthier business culture. Now let's add a fifth reason of employee dissatisfaction. Author Melissa Llarenaof *Career Outcomes Matter* reports even higher numbers, particularly for Generation X employees. She cites the biggest reason for "quits" is that employees no longer trust corporations. To wit, nearly 40 percent of men and 25 percent of women want to become their own boss, she says (54% of Millenials, 46% of GenY, 35% of Gen X-ers and 21% of Baby Boomers, by age).

Do you see what I'm seeing? Corporate employees are looking for a better working environment. Is this alarming? It should be to managers who need a talented team to accomplish corporate goals. The answer to employees saying, "I'm outta here!" is for management to thoughtfully and sincerely establish an employee-focused culture. Instead of leaving without direction here's a blue print to get you started.

BYOB PRINCIPLE if you don't make the time you'll never do it in time

Time is an equal opportunity employer. Each human being has exactly the same number of hours and minutes every day. Rich people can't buy more hours. Scientists can't invent new minutes. And you can't save time to spend it on another day. Even so, time is amazingly fair and forgiving. No matter how much time you've wasted in the past, you still have an entire tomorrow."
— Denis Waitley
The hardest thing about being an entrepreneur is BYOB while working full time..It feels like you're suffocating all of your creative genius on hold until 5pm quitting time. Mundane meetings, conference calls, action plans seem to be never ending. Assuming you have an idea of what you want to do there is something you can do:

1. **Decide what your intentions toward your assignment** To everything *there is* a season, and a time to every purpose under the heaven: Ecclesiastes 11:1

- I intend to start living a much more frugal lifestyle so I can create a savings account and have a financial buffer when I do quit my job and start running my own company
- I intend to come home from work, spend two hours with <u>my family</u>, then spend three hours working on my new business

- I intend to completely disconnect myself from my 9-5 job when I leave my 9-5 job, when you start making time toward your startup don't dive in head first, gradually transition one hour at a time until your doing a full 3 hours toward your business.
- My Intentions toward my assignment:_____
_____
_____
_____
_____
_

2. **Find your rhythm** :Do you work well late at night or early in the morning? Is it best for you to get more sleep during the week and dedicate weekends to your startup? Create a lifestyle that works for you. Stress and lack of sleep can do a number on your immune system. Make sure that you are eating well, getting exercise, and reviving yourself every once in a while with a break. "So teach [us] to number our days, that we may apply [our] hearts unto wisdom". Psalm 90:12

- I will find my rhythm by:_____
_____
_____
_____
_____
_____

3. **Forget the Trip and focus on the Journey**: Your job is just as important as your assignment (purpose). They're going to be many people calling for your help , but don't get distracted set an agenda, put everyone on a schedule . don't work over 12 hours a day, 8 hours for your job 1hr for restoration , that leaves 3 hours 1 hour for friends task and 2 hours to work strictly on your stuff, send all calls to voicemail "Redeeming the time, because the days are evil". Ephesians 5:16

- I will no longer let my day get away from me
- Doing my best doesn't mean without REST
- I will START following a schedule

CHAPTER FOUR CAREER JUICE

Career Juice

Before you go on the hunt, you need to prepare and follow up through e-mail, phone, and fax **Daily.** Show up once a week, **not during peak periods.**

Highlight: Goals, Experience, Strengths, & Expectations
Know what goals you want to achieve, personal and professional, and highlight the most experience that qualifies you for the job. What strengths make you an asset to the company and what expectations do you have for you and the company?

Utilize: all resources until you find a job
Billboards, newspapers, Internet, church, and volunteer.

Network: make yourself known so others can recognize you, link with others through committees, and ask for advice to help you on your search

Train for the interview and presenting the application through role-play
"And the LORD answered me, and said, Write the vision, and make [it] plain upon tables, that he may run that readeth it" Habakkuk 2:2.

~~Career Juice~~

12 steps to a higher level - it's not just a job, but also a career.

Ask– Questions about the job description; this shows interest

Never ask about the wage until a hiring decision is made

Professional– Attitude and outlook. You can't dress for the job; you have to get the career you want, and don't be pushy.

Proof- Provide documents (awards, letters of recommendation) for character reference.

** Don't lie your way through to the interview** It will cost you the job!

List- References, achievements, and hobbies.

Always call your references so they get a heads up. Also, when you list these things that others tend to overlook, it gives the manager an idea of your character.

Ink- Make sure you fill out your application in blue or black not red ink and no pencil.

Complete- when you leave blanks, you open yourself up to questions.

Check your spelling please

Availability– you should be flexible.

Talk- Please you have to stay positive with a vision; don't forget to use your highlights.

Instructions- Whatever they tell you to do during the application process,

it's very important that you do it.

Omissions- can keep you from the job as well; have some integrity.

Answer why you left the job or if you have a felony truthfully.

Neat- how your application looks will determine the company's outlook; if they hire you!

"Ye have not chosen me, but I have chosen you, and ordained you, that ye should go and bring forth fruit, and [that] your fruit should remain: that whatsoever ye shall ask of the Father in my name, he may give it you" John 15:16.

~~Career juice~~

Some Tips to consider when writing a resume

Research- gather facts about the company and job description so you can tailor your resume to fit the company.

Employment history/skills- needs to be chronological and accurate. Most managers are looking for stability and experience. if your history is sporadic focus on the job skills acquired from each job.

Syntax {grammar}- Use complete sentences that express a complete thought. Use action verbs do not write in first person.

This needs to be updated often, every promotion, any time there is a change in your employment status.

Mission statement- What you expect and what you will do for the company.

Education- is helpful when it complements the field you're applying for.

Specific– Get to the point and keep it on one page.

"In all labour there is profit: but the talk of the lips [tendeth] only to penury" **Proverbs 14:23.**

~~Career juice~~

Things we forget when we gain employment!!

Energy- Are you getting the proper rest, so when you arrive to work, you can set the pace?

Morals- Are you checking to see what's right more than being right?
"And whatsoever ye do, do [it] heartily, as to the Lord, and not unto men" **Col. 3:23**

Procedure- Are you submitting to the rules on your job?

Listen & Learn- are you listening before you speak to enhance the learning process?

Order- Are you following the chain of authority and prioritizing your day?

Yield learns- what your limits are and exercise them carefully.

Ministry– Doesn't stop at the end of church service. Take it to work with you.

The closer you get to God, the higher you will go. After all, He is the Most High.

"Brethren, let every man, wherein he is called, therein abide with God" I Cor. 7:24

Enthusiasm- are you a positive influence on your job?

Necessity– Become an expert in your field; study all facets of your field so you become the point person for that company.

Time- Time is money, so be on time and complete assignments on time.

"But I rejoiced in the Lord greatly, that now at the last your care of me hath flourished again; wherein ye were also careful, but ye lacked opportunity. Not that I speak in respect of want: for I have learned, in whatsoever state I am, [therewith] to be content." Philippians 4:10-11

~~Career juice~~

When considering leaving a job, consider these four principles:

Justice: Is there fairness where you work?

Opportunity: Is their opportunity for you to move to the next level that does not interfere with home life?

Benefits: Does the company provide benefits to you and your family?

Satisfied: Are you satisfied 90% of the time with your work place?

~~Career juice~~

"Promotion begin from the inside out"

Punctual = Psalms 90:12

Respectful=Hebrews 13:17

Objectives=Proverbs 24:27

Morals=1st Corinthians 15:33

Organization= 1st Corinthians 14:40

Training=2 Timothy 2:15

Initiative= Proverbs 22:29

Observation= Luke 11:34

Network= Romans 10:18

~~Career juice~~

"Assignments don't create status; but they can build stature upon completion"

Attitude =Philippians 2:14

Skill Set= Ecclesiastes 9:11

Submission= Romans 13:1-2

Instructions = Proverbs 15:32

Goal **O**riented=Ezekiel 11:19-20

Negotiable = Amos 3:3

Model= 2 Corinthians 7:2

Education= Ecclesiastes 1:16

Name=Proverbs 22:1

Teamwork=Proverbs 27:17

Coach's Corner

"Your assignment is not your decision; it's your assessment for promotion" `

There are many of us who seek promotion from our current assignment. Unfortunately until our stature changes our status remains the same. I remember I had begun a fast that week and the car broke down. So I called my brother in the ministry and he allowed us to borrow the church van. He was teaching a series about passing the test. so i decided to fast and make that my assignment to which was passing the test, that was my total focus! The funny thing is your assignment is not your decision it's your discovery- Mike Murdock.

I discovered that I couldn't passed the test until I discovered why they existed. So the first day with the church van I'm gassing & breaking because I didn't follow the Pastor explicit instructions to let the van sit for forty five minutes I tried to crank and Go so that day I failed, the second day I realized I was on trial the first day but still was being tried so I said I'll do better but I failed that day too because the driver ran over the neighbor's garbage cans which took me was in a whole other zip code. I was having a whole conversation ; but after I saw her face I said accidents happen, 20 min later we ran out of Gas, I failed this day too because i lost my patience ,the third day I realized I would stay on **trial** until i **endured** that same day the battery died ; but I was determined not to fail again then something amazing took place I became **stronger,** now i *have a* *testimony* now I'm **enlightened** ,the most important thing i learned is you have to be **discipline**

But they must first be tested. Then, if they prove to be blameless(innocent of wrongdoing), let them serve in ministry(vocation/Leadership). 1 Timothy 3:10

T- Trial   Ps. 119:74 Kjv
E- Endure   Matt. 24:13
S- Strengthen   1 Peter 5:10
T - Testimony   Revelation 12:11
E - Enlightenment - John 3:19   , James 4:17
D - Discipline Hebrews 12:7 NLT

Please look up scriptures so that you can understand where the fit in your life

CHAPTER FIVE MASTER APPLICATION

1. Filling out an application can be difficult and time consuming if you have no experience. References, awards, and letters of recommendations can help you.
2. Months, dates, and years are important. Always remember, when you start and end a job; this helps them know your tenure (how long you intend to keep the job).
3. Always give notice when you intend to leave a job. This shows respect, and it also leaves a door open in case you have to go back.
4. Blanks leave room for questions, and they also indicate you have something to hide.

Personal information

Name: _____
Phone_____
Address: _____ Social
Security_____
City: _____ State: _____
Zip:_____
Isaiah 3:10Say ye to the righteous, that [it shall be] well [with him]: for they shall eat the fruit of their doings.
(your personal info tells us were you've been and possibly where you could take us)

Education:

School Name: _____ Last grade completed:_____
Address: _____ Years attended:_____
Course of study: _____ Degree:_____

Proverbs 18:15   The heart of the prudent getteth knowledge; and the ear of the wise seeketh knowledge.
(people who have been taught in school are easier to train sometimes)

Would you work?   (FT)   (PT)

What is your availability?

Sunday	Monday	Tuesday	Wednesday	Thursday	Friday	Saturday

five *Psalms 90:12   So teach [us] to number our days, that we may apply [our] hearts unto wisdom.*

(You can schedule around your life if we know your availability)

MASTER APPLICATION II

When can you start work?
_____

Are there any skills or qualifications which you feel will especially fit you to work with our organization?

_____

Do you have a felony? _____ If yes, please explain_____

_____

_____

_____**Do you have a
reliable way to work?**

_____

Proverbs 18:16
A man's gift maketh room for him, and bringeth him before great men.
(What benefits do you bring to the table?)

Experience

Employer:

_____

Supervisor:

_____

Job title:

_____

Duties:

_____

Telephone
#:_____

Address:

_____

Salary or wage:

_____

Dates employed:

_____

Reason for leaving:

_____

Employer:

_____

Supervisor:

_____

Job title:

_____

Duties:

_____

Telephone
#:_____

Address:

_____

Salary or wage:

_____

Dates employed:

_____

Reason for leaving:

_____

II Corinthians 8:3
for I bear witness that according to their ability, yes, and beyond their ability, they were freely willing
(is your experience applicable for the job your applying for)

MASTER APPLICATION III REFRENCES NOT RELATIVES

Name: _____

Phone: _____

Address: _____

Occupation: _____

Three references total please.

Three steps to meeting the Manager

(A. T. & T.)

Let's make connections that count

Ask

1. For the name of the Manager
2. To speak to the Manager
3. Ask for the interview
4. For the application if they can't interview you
* When is an appropriate time to see & talk to a manager?

Tell

1. How much you desire to work for the company
2. How you intend to help their company grow as well as how it can help you
3. When you will be able to start

Thank

1. The manager with a letter
2. The manager by telephone, and ask them what you need to do to qualify for their next opening

Proverbs 18:24

A man [that hath] friends must show himself friendly: and there is a friend [that] sticketh closer than a brother.

Resume Format

I Corinthians 14:40
Let all things be done decently and in order.

Name: _____

Address:_____

City, State, &

Zip_____

Phone:

_____

Objective:

Ecclesiastes 3:1 To every [thing there is] a season, and a time to every

purpose under the heaven.

To partner with a company that possesses honesty and integrity, which fosters open communication among the team, and where opportunity is based on results.

Work experience:

Romans 12:6-7

Having then gifts differing according to the grace that is given to us, whether prophecy, [let us prophesy] according to the proportion of faith;

12:7 Or ministry, [let us wait] on [our] ministering: or he that teaches, on teaching.

Circle K   05/24/2004- -05/26/2006

Senior training manager

Daily cash reconciliation, loss prevention, merchandising, training, and recruiting

Educational experience:

Hosea 4:6

My people are destroyed for lack of knowledge: because thou hast rejected knowledge, I will also reject thee, that thou shalt be no priest to me: seeing thou hast forgotten the law of thy God, I will also forget thy children.

Florida Metropolitan University 05/24/1991 06/25/2002
Criminal Justice

Cover letter format

Date
Manger's name
Name of the company
Address
City, State, and Zip

Dear ( ):

Tell how you learned of the position.

Tell what makes you qualified for the job.

In closing, include your phone number and when you will contact them or meet with them. Last but not least, thank them for the opportunity to be a part of their team.

Sincerely,

Your name
Address
City, state, & Zip
Telephone number

Ecclesiastes 7:1
A good name [is] better than precious ointment; and the day of death than the day of one's birth.

Controlling the interview

Open: With I.n.t.r.o.

Initiate contact by using employer's name

Now introduce yourself and shake his/her hand

Tell them the position you qualify for and why

Remember to smile and keep eye contact

Offer application and or resume

Close: F.u.s.e.

Firm & friendly handshake

Use employer's name

Say thank you for their time and the opportunity

Explain that you're really looking forward to working with them

Proverbs29: 20
Seest thou a man [that is] hasty in his words? [There is] more hope of a fool than of him.
Proverbs28: 13
He that covereth his sins shall not prosper: but whoso confesseth and forsaketh [them] shall have mercy.

Insert The Inquisition Quest (Interview Questions)

1. Tell me about yourself?

Employers want to know if they will like you. To be on point, you need to write a thirty-second commercial that includes positive, practical information and work history.

2. Do you smoke?

I tolerate smoking, but appreciate a smoke free work environment.

3. What do you know about the company?

Be sure you know about the company and the position you're applying for.

4. What do you hope to be doing in 2, 4, or 6 years from now?

This question is asked to see if you have long-term or short-term goals
for their company

5. What is your starting wage or salary?

What do you pay someone with my experience or what is the pay for this position?

6. What is your biggest weakness? {Isaiah 40:29}

Never admit a weakness; instead turn a weakness into strength
(i.e. Some people say I talk too much; but I just love people and feel the more you get to know them the better service you can provide).
Or you can turn strengths into weaknesses

(I'm a fanatic about being on time; sometimes it drives people crazy that I'm always early).
7. What will your references say about you?
Probably nothing if you forget to call them and get their permission. Never take a chance; you might chance yourself out of a job.

I Peter 3:15 "But sanctify the Lord God in your hearts and be ready always to give an answer to every man that asketh you a reason of hope that is in you with meekness and fear"

Employer Search and Rescue List

Telephone Date & time	Type of job Where was it advertised	Name of contact and position	Results	Comments

Luke 11:9-10

And I say unto you, Ask, and it shall be given you; seek, and ye shall find; knock, and it shall be opened unto you.
For every one that asketh receiveth; and he that seeketh findeth; and to him that knocketh it shall be opened.

Godly Talking Encourages

GTE, Taking conversation to a higher level!!!

- *We are fully responsible for every word we say.*
"But I say unto you, That every idle word that men shall speak, they shall give account thereof in the day of judgment." Matthew 12:36
- *The tongue always reveals your heart*
"O generation of vipers, how can ye, being evil, speak good things? For out of the abundance of the heart the mouth speaketh." Matthew 12:34
- *Just because words are smooth as butter, don't forget that butter can be hard sometimes*
"[The words] of his mouth were smoother than butter, but war [was] in his heart: his words were softer than oil, yet [were] they drawn swords." Psalm 55:21

Twelve disciplines of talking:
1. *"He that keepeth his mouth keepeth his life, but he that openeth wide his lips shall have destruction" Proverbs13:3*
2. *"Seest though a man that is hasty in his words? There is more hope for a fool than him" Proverbs 29:20*
3. *"He that answerth a matter before he heareth it' it is folly and shame unto him" Proverbs 18:13*
4. *"... every idle word that men shall speak. They shall give account of it in the day of judgement" Matthew12:36*

5. *"Let no corrupt communication proceed out of your mouth, but that which is good to the use of edifying, that it may minister grace unto the hearers" Ephesians 4:29*

Godliness Talking Encourages II

6. *"Wherefore, my beloved brethren, let every man be swift to hear, slow to speak, slow to wrath" James 1:19*
7. *"Whoso keepeth his mouth and his tongue his soul from troubles" Proverbs 21:23*
8. *" a soft answer turneth away wrath: but grievous words stir up anger... a wholesome tongue is a tree of life" Proverbs 15:1-4*
9. *"Even a fool, when he holdeth his peace, is counted wise: and he that shutteth his lips is esteemed a man of understanding" Proverbs 17:28*
10. *"The light of the eyes rejoiceth the heart: [and] a good report maketh the bones fat" Proverbs 15:30*
11. *"For he that will love life, and see good days, let him refrain his tongue from evil, and his lips that they speak no guile" I Peter 3:10*
12. *"If any man among you seem to be religious, and bridleth not his tongue, but deceiveth his own heart, this man's religion [is] vain" James 1:26*

Job offer questionnaire!

We as faithful stewards need to stop selling ourselves short. Do you feel that because you're applying for a job, you can't ask questions? "You will never reach the finish line, if you do not approach the starting line" Michael Gatewood. The bible says: ***But by what means he now seeth, we know not; or who hath opened his eyes, we know not: he is of age; ask him: he shall speak for himself. John 9:21***

1. When would you like for me to begin?

2. Where will I work?

3. What are my hours?

4. What kind of training will I receive?

5. What is the starting salary for someone in this field? You can always go to www.salary.com to get an idea.

6. What can I do to advance in the company?

7. What are the benefits this company has to offer?

CHAPTER SIX THE INTERVIEW

Fan Relationship   Mark 9:41 Hebrews 13:2

"For whosoever shall give you a cup of water to drink in my name, because ye belong to Christ, verily I say unto you, he shall not lose his reward."
"Be not forgetful to entertain strangers: for thereby some have entertained angels unawares"

Tell me about a time when someone complained to you. How did you handle the situation?

Tell me more about a time when you had to deal with an irate fan. What did you do?

Attention to Detail   Proverbs 10:4 Psalm 39:4-7

"He becometh poor that dealeth [with] a slack hand: but the hand of the diligent maketh rich"

Tell me about a task or project for which you were responsible.

What did you do to get it done completely, correctly, and on time?

Tolerance for Stress   Galatians 6:9   Joshua 1:9

"And let us not be weary in well doing: for in due season we shall reap, if we faint not"

"Have not I commanded thee? Be strong and of a good courage; be not afraid, neither be thou dismayed: for the LORD thy God [is] with thee whithersoever thou goest"

What types of situations do you find frustrating on the field?

Under what conditions do you play best?

Co-Operation   Ecclesiastes 4:9-12

Tell me more about a time when you had to work with another person.

Tell me more about a time when you were on a team. What did you do?

Dependability   Titus 1:7-9

If I call your previous coach, what would they say about your attendance record?

Tell me about a situation when you had to complete a project with little or no supervision. How did you complete the project?

Other Considerations

*Show the player the position requirements and ask is there any reason that they cannot perform any of the position requirements.
►If they say yes, record their exceptions and let the team owner know.

Second Interview

Fan Relationship   Matthew 5:6

"Blessed [are] they which do hunger and thirst after righteousness: for they shall be filled"

Tell me about the time when someone complained to you?

How did you handle it?

Attention to Detail   Hebrews 13:17

"Obey them that have the rule over you, and submit yourselves: for they watch for your souls, as they that must give account, that they may do it with joy, and not with grief: for that [is] unprofitable for you"

Tell me about a situation in which you had to follow a detailed set of instructions to complete a project.

Tolerance for Stress   Philippians 4:6, 13

"Be careful for nothing; but in every thing by prayer and supplication with thanksgiving let your requests be made known unto God"
"I can do all things through Christ which strengtheneth me"

Tell me about a situation when you had to work together with someone?

What did you do?

Co- Operation   Colossians: 4:6

"Let your speech [be] alway with grace, seasoned with salt, that ye may know how ye ought to answer every man"

Tell me about a time when you had to play hard with others to complete a task. Describe how you interacted with them.

Dependability   Psalm 37:3

"Trust in the LORD, and do good; [so] shalt thou dwell in the land, and verily thou shalt be fed."

Tell me about a time when someone asked you to break a commitment. What did you do?

Summary

Rate the player's interview based on response
►Team History - 3 points
►Appearance - 2 points
►Fan Relations - 3 points
►Attention to Detail - 4 points
►Tolerance for Stress - 3 points
►Cooperation - 3 points
►Dependability - 3 points
If you have more negatives than positives,
remember - MVPs are
hired, rarely inspired.

Notes

TEAM PLAYER EXIT INTERVIEW

Instructions: Write the number that best describes how you feel next to each question. For each reason that challenges you to leave a job, create an opportunity to stay on your new job.

1 STRONGLY DISAGREE	2 DISAGREE	3 NEITHER	4 AGREE	5 STRONGLY AGREE

Reason for leaving:
1. I have accepted another job for more money.
2. The job was not what I expected it to be.
    (Please give comments below)
3. I have accepted another job with better career opportunities.
4. I am returning to school full time.

Working Conditions:
1. My work schedules were prepared fairly.
2. I received the right amount of hours.
3. The office was well maintained and comfortable.
4. I was treated fairly.
5. I feel that this is a good place to work.
6. The job itself is the main reason I am leaving.
    (Please give detail below)

Management Support:

1. I had a good relationship with my managers.
2. Overall, I was satisfied with management.
3. Overall, I was satisfied with the training I received.
4. A problem with management is my main reason for leaving.

Company Policies:
   All necessary policies and procedures were explained to me
1. Policies and procedures were always followed.
   1.

Comments:

_____

_____

_____

CHAPTER SEVEN JOBS IN THE BIBLE

The following is a listing of occupations mentioned in the Bible. Have a career day to help the children learn about the different kinds of jobs held by people during biblical times. Write on a sheet of paper the occupation and a brief description of that occupation; also write the salary this person should be making from start to finish.

Job	Reference
Ambassador	2 Corinthians 5:20
Archer	Genesis 21:20
Armor-bearer	Judges 9:54
Astrologer	Isaiah 47:13
Athlete	2 Timothy 2:5
Baker	Genesis 40:1
Bandit	Hosea 7:1
Banker	Matthew 25:27
Blacksmith	1 Samuel 13:19

Barber	Ezekiel 5:1
Bodyguard	1 Samuel 28:2
Bowmen	Isaiah 21:17
Brick maker	Genesis 11:3
Builder	2 Kings 12:11
Butcher	Matthew 22:4
Carpenter	Mark 6:3; Matt. 13:55
Carver	Exodus 31:5
Chariot driver	1 Kings 22:34
Charioteer	1 Chronicles 19:18
Cook	1 Samuel 8:13
Counselor	2 Samuel 15:12
Courier	2 Chronicles 30:6
Creditor	Deuteronomy 15:2
Designer	Exodus 35:35
Diviner	1 Samuel 6:2
Doorkeeper	2 Kings 22:4
Embalmer	Gen. 50:26
Embroiderer	Exodus 35:35
Emperor	Acts 25:25
Engraver	Exodus 28:11
Executioner	Mark 6:27
Farmer	2 Timothy 2:6

Fisherman	Isaiah 19:8
Fortuneteller	Acts 16:16
Gardener	John 20:15
Gatekeeper	2 Samuel 18:26
Gem cutter	Exodus 28:11
Goldsmith	Isaiah 40:19
Governor	2 Kings 23:8
Grape picker	Jeremiah 49:9
Grinder	Ecclesiastes 12:3
Guard	1 Samuel 22:17
Harpist	Revelation 14:2
Harvester	James 5:4
Herdsmen	Genesis 13:7
Horseman	2 Kings 9:17
Hunter	Genesis 10:9
Idol maker	Isaiah 45:16
Innkeeper	Luke 10:35
Instructor	Proverbs 5:13
Interpreter	Genesis 42:23
Jailer	Acts 16:23
Judge	Exodus 2:14
Keeper of flocks	Genesis 4:2
King	Genesis 14:1

Landowner	Matthew 20:1
Lawyer	Acts 24:1
Magician	Daniel 2:10
Magistrate	Luke 12:58
Maidservant	Deuteronomy 15:17
Manservant	Exodus 20:10
Mason	2 Kings 12:12
Merchant	Matthew 13:45
Messenger	1 Samuel 23:27
Metal forger	Genesis 4:22
Midwife	Genesis 35:17
Minister	Isaiah 61:6
Moneylender	Exodus 22:25
Musician	Psalms 68:25
Oarsmen	Ezekiel 27:8
Officer	1 Chronicles 26:24
Overseer	Acts 20:28
Perfumer	1 Samuel 8:13
Pharmacist	Exodus 37:29
Philosopher	Acts 17:18
Physician	Jeremiah 8:22
Planter	Amos 9:13
Plowman	Amos 9:13

Poet	Acts 17:28
Potter	Isaiah 29:16
Preacher	2 Peter 2:5
Priest	Genesis 14:18
Proconsul	Acts 13:7
Prophet	Genesis 20:7
Queen	1 Kings 10:1
Rabbi	Matthew 23:7
Reaper	2 Kings 4:18
Refiner	Malachi 3:3
Robber	John 10:1
Satrap	Ezra 8:36
Scribe	1 Chronicles 24:6
Seer	1 Samuel 9:9
Servant	Genesis 15:3
Sheepshearer	2 Samuel 13:23
Shepherd	1 Samuel 21:7
Silversmith	Judges 17:4
Slave	Genesis 44:10
Soldier	John 19:23
Spy	Numbers 21:32
Steward	Genesis 43:16
Stonecutter	2 Kings 12:12

Stonemason	2 Samuel 5:11
Swordsman	2 Kings 3:26
Tax collector	Matthew 10:3
Tailor	Exodus 39:1
Teacher	1 Chronicles 25:8
Tentmaker	Acts 18:3
Treasurer	Ezra 1:8
Trumpeter	2 Kings 11:14
Vine grower	Joel 1:11
Warrior	Judges 11:1
Watchman	2 Samuel 13:34
Water carrier	Joshua 9:21
Weaver	Exodus 35:35
Woodcutter	Joshua 9:21
Woodsman	2 Chronicles 2:10
Writer	Psalms 45:1

. "A Man out of work is a man out oif ideas" BYOB Principle

Jobs of the Bible Worksheet

Please write your research from the jobs of the bible on this page.

Job Assignment	Job Description	JobSalary

Job Assignment	Job Description	Job Salary

Job Assignment	Job Description	Job Salary

8 CHAPTER EIGHT CAREER
SUCCESS AGREEMENT & EVALUATION

Career Success Agreement

When you sign this agreement focus on the issues, recognize your good days and accomplishments, this is not a things to do book, this is record of your journey as a solider for Christ, your mission is to tear down strong holds in the work place. Your aim is to convert and convict the carnal minded, to pursue a life with Christ. Your promise is to record your thoughts every day in hopes that you will express what you feel rather than explode when you feel. If you accept this mission you must support the C.R.E.A.M principle(s) {Christ Rules Every Thing Around Me}

> ➤ He must increase, but I [must] decrease. John 3:30

> ➤ And no man taketh this honour unto himself, but he that is called of God, as [was] Aaron. Hebrews 5:4

> ➤ And I thank Christ Jesus our Lord, who hath enabled me, for that he counted me faithful, putting me into the ministry 1st Timothy 1:12

> ➤ Create in me a clean heart, O God; and renew a right spirit within me. Psalm 51:10

> ➤ Study to show thyself approved unto God, a workman that needeth not to be ashamed, rightly dividing the word of truth. 2nd Timothy 2:15

> ➤ Honour thy father and [thy] mother: and, Thou shalt love thy neighbour as thyself. Matthew 19:19

> ➤ And as ye would that men should do to you, do ye also to them likewise. Luke 6:31

I_____ Accept the

charge and the one hundred **Career Success Points** in this book on

the _____ of _____, _____. And commit my self

to excellence in the work place & making my work space a

worship place.

C.R.E.A.M. EVALUATION

Please put a X by the quotes that apply to you. If more than three are left blank you have some work to do.

	"Half of nothing is still nothing" Rick Patterson
	Many people quit looking for work when they find a job. *~Author Unknown*
	"If you have a job without any aggravations, you don't have a job".~Malcolm S. Forbes
	. Don't waste time learning the "tricks of the trade." *Instead, learn the trade.* *~Attributed to both James Charlton and H. Jackson Brown, Jr.*
	You're no good unless you are a good assistant; and if you are, you're too good to be an assistant. ~Martin H. Fischer
	There are no menial jobs, only menial attitudes. *~William J. Bennett*
	The difference between a job and a career is the difference between forty and sixty hours a week. ~Robert Frost

	It is not titles that honor men, but men that honor titles. *~Niccolo Machiavelli*
	A memorandum is written not to inform the reader but to protect the writer.~Dean Acheson
	"Search others for their virtue, and yourself for your vices." *~R. Buckminster Fuller*
	"A good leader is not the person who does things right, but the person who finds the right things to do."~Anthony T. Dadovano
	"Your work should be your passion.... not your prison."~author Unknown
	"Wise people learn when they can. Fools learn when they must."~Wellington
	"For everyone who exalts himself will be humbled, and he who humbles himself will be exalted."~From the Gospel of Luke
	"Nothing is really work unless you would rather be doing something else"~James M. Barrie
	Nothing worthwhile comes easily. Work, continuous work and hard work, is the only way to accomplish results that last.~ Hamilton Holt
	"A person who likes to be seen; is often seen doing nothing" ~ Pastor Patrick Thompson
	"One important key to success is self confidence. An important key to self confidence is preparation"~ Arthur Ashe
	Only undertake what you can do in an excellent fashion. There are no prizes for average performance. ~Brian Tracy
	"Opportunity is missed by most people because it is dressed in overalls and looks like work"~Thomas Edison

"you can't profess what you do not possess" *~ Pastor Patrick Thompson*
Our talents are God's gift to us: What we make of our talents is our gift back to God. ~Leo Buscaglia
. Our work is the presentation of our Preparation. ~ *Michael Gatewood*
"You would not be board if you are busy" *~ Michael Gatewood*
"Nothing is particularly hard if you divide it in to small jobs" ~ Henry Ford
"Persistence is the key to overcoming the lock of resistance"~ Michael Gatewood
"Think like a wise man, but communicate in the language of people" *William Butler Yeats*
"You can't escape responsibility of tomorrow by evading it today" ~Abraham Lincoln
"The Trouble with the rat race is even when you win your still a rat" *~ Lilly Tomlin*
"Stop looking at wear your at and start watching where you're going" *~Kenneth Perry(cab driver & my Friend)*
"The sweetness of the lips increaseth learning" Proverbs 16:21
"Confess [your] faults one to another, and pray one for another, that ye may be healed. The effectual fervent prayer of a righteous man availeth much" James 5:16.

	"And we know that all things work together for good to them that love God, to them who are the called according to [his] purpose" Romans 8:28.
	" You may not be rewarded for your strengths, but you will be disqualified for your weakness" ~Dr. Robb Thompson
	" Information without instruction equals destruction" ~ Michael Gatewood
	"If you will not learn when some one instructs you, you will only complain when consequences attempt to teach you" ~ Dr. Robb Thompson
	"Vision without action is a day dream, Action without vision is a nightmare" ~ Japanese Proverb
	"If you can't run walk, if you can't walk crawl, if you can't crawl creep ,& if you can't creep just keep moving" ~ Pastor Patrick Thompson
	"Never live in the past, but always learn from it" ~Anonymous
	"To attempt to climb- to achieve – without a firm objective in life is to attain nothing"~Mary Robbing
	"Knowing is not enough we must apply, willing is not enough we must do" ~ Goethe
	"Knowing is not enough we must apply, willing is not enough we must do" ~ Goethe
	"We don't see things as they are, we see things as we are" Anais Nin
	"Only he who does nothing makes no mistake" French Proverb
	"Ajob done well ;is a job well done"~Michael Gatewood

	" A Position shouldn't confine you, it just defines what you do"~ Michael Gatewood
	If you have a job without any aggravations, you don't have a job. *~Malcolm S. Forbes*
	"Some people become successful because they are destined and most people become successful because they decide to be" ~ Michael Gatewood
	"It is not titles that honor men, but the deeds that accompany them" *~Michael Gatewood*
	A memorandum is written not to inform the reader but to protect the writer. ~Dean Acheson
	The best time to start thinking about your retirement is before the boss does. ~Author Unknown
	"A good leader is not the person who does things right, but the person who finds the right things to do." Anthony T. Dadovano
	"The issue with items that are free it reduces your freedom to negotiate" ~Michael Gatewood
	"The work will always be harder, when you hardly work"~Michael Gatewood

Assignment Evaluation

Category	Questions	Scripture Guide	Commentary
Attitude: a physical posture, either conscious or unconscious, specially while interacting with others, an opinion or general feeling about something	Do you Complain often? Are you Argumentative?	Philippians 2:14 Do all things without murmurings and disputings:	Attitude affects moral and often times productivity.
Skill Set: the ability to do something well,	How much time have you put in? Are you	Ecclesiastes 9:11 I returned,	There are times when skill and will

usually gained through training or experience	working to the best of your ability? Are you able to work without supervision? Are you able to teach others?	and saw under the sun, that the race [is] not to the swift, nor the battle to the strong, neither yet bread to the wise, nor yet riches to men of understanding, nor yet favour to men of skill; but time and chance happeneth to them all.	don't matter. Sometimes it Tenure or just because taking a chance on you! Moses spent 40 years in the wilderness preparing .how much time have you spent on your current assignment?
Submission: a willingness to yield or surrender to somebody, or the act of doing so	Will you take directions from someone? If there is a misunderstanding; are you the first to compromise?	Romans 13:1-2 Let every soul be subject unto the higher powers. For there is no power but of God: the powers that	Everybody has to answer to someone that is the way the chain of authority works. If you are not willing to

		be are ordained of God....	give an answer for the hope that is within you, choosing you for this assignment would be questionabl e.
Instruction (s) a spoken or written statement of what must be done, especially delivered formally, with official authority, or as an order	How many times must you be asked before you comply? Can you teach others in a way that makes them want to learn from you?	Proverbs 15:32 He that refuseth instruction despiseth his own soul: but he that heareth reproof getteth understandi ng.	A person who does not listen is void of understandi ng

GO (Goal-Oriented) Something that somebody wants to achieve openly supporting or favoring a particular point of view or set of beliefs	Are you a self-starter? Are you consistent? What is the difference between Productivity and Activity? Do you do what you say?	Ezekiel 11:19-20 And I will give them one heart, and I will put a new spirit within you; and I will take the stony heart out of their flesh, and will give them an heart of flesh...	Can't be double-minded you will never get anywhere and you will frustrate those around you because nothing is being accomplished.
Negotiable : not fixed but able to be established or changed through discussion and compromise	Are you willing to compromise? Why or why not? Are you ready to deal with change? you have to be willing to negotiate in order to navigate through change successfully	Amos 3:3 Can two walk together, except they be agreed? Come now, and let us reason together, saith the LORD: though your sins be as scarlet, they	Stubborn people create stumbling blocks because their heart is of stone their head becomes hard!

		shall be as white as snow; though they be red like crimson, they shall be as wool. See also Isaiah 1:18	
Model: an excellent example that deserves to be imitated	Are you setting an example? Are you letting your light shine before men? Who do you know is willing to follow your example?	2 Corinthians 7:2 Receive us; we have wronged no man, we have corrupted no man, we have defrauded no man.	"People who make examples of others; hardly follow an example themselves "People often mind what you do and remind you of what you say Paul said "follow me as I follow Christ"

Education: the imparting and acquiring of knowledge through teaching and learning, especially at a school or similar institution; training and instruction in a particular subject	What high school did you graduate from? Did you go to college? Is this your area of expertise?	Ecclesiastes 1:16 I communed with mine own heart, saying, Lo, I am come to great estate, and have gotten more wisdom than all [they] that have been before me in Jerusalem: yea, my heart had great experience of wisdom and knowledge.	Having an education proves you can complete something. It also may be a major qualifier for the assignment you are undertaking.

Name a word, term, or phrase by which somebody or something is known and distinguished from other people or things	What do people say about you? Do you care about what is being said?	Proverbs 22:1 A [good] name [is] rather to be chosen than great riches, [and] loving favour rather than silver and gold.	We have to keep a good reputation because we are representatives of an organization
Team Work a group of people forming one side in a sports competition	Do you work better in a group or by yourself? Do you understand collaborative learning?	Proverbs 27:17 Iron sharpeneth iron; so a man sharpeneth the countenance of his friend.	Sometimes you have to Go along to get along in the process you could develop each other.

THE MAN MICHAEL GATEWOOD

> ➤ 1987 Certified as Literature Evangelist by the South Eastern Conference of Seventh Day Adventist

> ➤ 2009 Graduated from Grace & Truth Christian University , Theology Major

> ➤ 2014 Pastor of Gracesons Life Class International and Host of Lifeline. He is an effective communicator of the truth about how people can rise above their perceived limitations. Michael Gatewood is a man of driven faith who believes he can do all things through Christ who strengthens him. He shares his heart via Lifeline, a conference call program for, entrepreneurs and ministries.

> ➤ 2015 Shared The Stage With Earl Davis, Jr. 2002 Olympic Torch bearer, Bershawn Shaw, Life Coach & Motivational Speaker at The SWAG Women's Conference

> ➤ He is a skilled Executive Coach whose charismatic flair invigorates the room. Gatewood served as a corporate trainer for an international restaurant chain and

developed tools to turn a store in sight of closure into a $4M profitable business.

➤ The author of Coaching the Uncoachable, Coaching the Unemployable, and Michael Gatewood's Will Power Journal, he wrote, "All of my life people kept telling me how good I could be at certain things, but nobody gave me a roadmap. This is my way of teaching others practical ways on how to become great."

➤ Former President of the Florida Independent Living Association (for foster children).

➤ Realizing the high rate of unemployment in an area of Tampa, he partnered with a local pastor to conduct a series of workshops to teach the principles of decision making, effective communication, time management and dealing with difficult people—subjects covered in his books. He also wrote and performed in plays designed to empower and educate youth.

THE MINISTRY OF MICHAEL GATEWOOD

➤ Gracesons Life Class Int., is a community media ministry, which teaches life principles, based on the Word of God. Gracesons Life Class International uses technology for a collaborative learning experience teaching on family values, relationships, evangelism, employment, and entrepreneurship. Gracesons Life Class Int. is training the next generation for self-sufficiency through life classes. glci.study@gmail.com

> ➢ Tuesdays Lifeline @ 7pm A line for saving or preserving life. It is something regarded as indispensable for maintaining protection of life. for the entrepreneur going into business, we desire life line to be the resource that helps you get started. Ministries who desire to expand, lifeline will help you grow. Life line is a source that keeps you connected with resources available to you .The weekly training calls are progressive and responsive to requests from its participants. From the basics of how to get started through the advanced stages of expansion and restructuring, be connected to people who are connected to Truth and Integrity.

> .

> ➢ SWAT (Evangelistic Outreach Program Youth 1st & 2nd Thursday S.W.A.T. Youth Academy was established to enlighten our youth and empower them to be strong, courageous decision-makers for today, as well pioneers for the next generation. By providing a healthy platform for them to hear their heartbeat, and motivating each individual to discover and pursue his/her purpose, they will see themselves as a valuable member of the family unit and a viable citizen in the community.

> ➢ Man 2 Man (Men's Ministry) 1st & 2nd Saturday at 8pm (Is a place for men to connect him Man 2 Man seeks to sharpen and strengthen men through God's Word, fellowship, encouragement and support. The Man 2 Man is a multifaceted, comprehensive ministry that will expand the Kingdom of God by encouraging and supporting men to walk in their calling and purpose.

> ➢ Christian Lounge Friday nights 8pm. Is a place where young & old can connect and fellowship Heart & soul food A place of Rehabilitation through biblical principles and practical applications for a better life?

THE LEGACY OF MICHAEL GATEWOOD

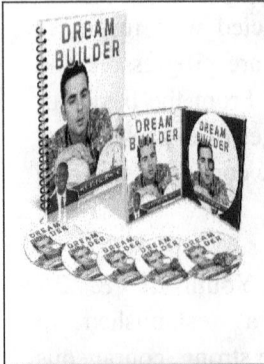	Dreams and visions are mentioned in the Bible, and God sometimes used the dream state to communicate with His prophets and others. God spoke to Abimelech in Genesis 20, warning him not to touch Abraham's wife, Sarah. Other dreams include Jacob's ladder (Genesis 28), Joseph's dream that his brothers would serve him that led to his captivity in Egypt (Genesis 37), $95.95 plus tax, s/h Free
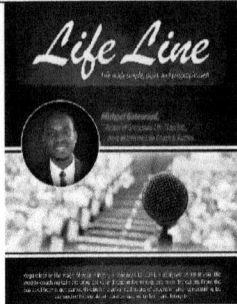	Lifeline coaching call, Godly principles made practical for you to enjoy life. Over 200 Conversations of dignitaries, entrepreneur in our library. Making life simple, plain, and uncomplicated please. Join Live us every Tuesday at 7pm 641-715-3850 code 890296147 contact us via website for more details www.michaelgatewoodslifeline.blogspotcom Or call our office for a catalog 954-358-9425 $8.95 plus tax , S/h Free
	Personal Development series on Life / Work /Leadership. During this series we've encouraged people to Experience life by dreaming big, Expect life by setting goals and Execute your life by taking action! This course is designed to help you succeed. It has been developed by Entrepreneurs, Ministers and Ceo's . This Series is based on the Word of God .Invest in your success today only $895.00 (includes 31 digital downloads and a workbook pdf, for the 31 cd's and a workbook an additional $100.00) call the office and order today 9543589425 orl mgpublication@gmail.com

MICHAEL GATEWOOD

BYOB ON A
$0 BUDGET

BUILDING YOUR OWN BUSINESS

For it is WRITTEN: "Wherefore he saith, When he ascended up on high, he led captivity captive, and gave gifts unto men". Ephesians 4:8 your circumstances don't have to hold you captive, capitalize during this economy with your gifts using **e**Commerce!

Find out how you will learn:

1. Tips for BYOB on a $0 Budget
2. Who has our money
3. Fifteen things my mentors taught me about money!
4 .personal rolodex of resources available to you
5. Three 30 min coaching sessions

$275.95 plus tax

SPECIAL OFFER

If you're looking for a job and you can't find one call my office I'll help you for free , I'll make you a resume and donate three hours of my time to you . this offer is only valid with proof of purchase.

www.ingramcontent.com/pod-product-compliance
Lightning Source LLC
Chambersburg PA
CBHW070815100426
42742CB00012B/2372